THE GREATEST STORIES
NEVER TOLD: SNIPERS

THE GREATEST STORIES NEVER TOLD: SNIPERS

LAURENCE J. YADON

LYONS
PRESS

Guilford, Connecticut

An imprint of The Rowman & Littlefield Publishing Group, Inc.
4501 Forbes Blvd., Ste. 200
Lanham, MD 20706
www.rowman.com

Distributed by NATIONAL BOOK NETWORK

British Library Cataloguing in Publication Information available

Library of Congress Cataloging-in-Publication Data available

ISBN 978-1-4930-3855-8 (paperback)
ISBN 978-1-4930-3856-5 (e-book)

∞™ The paper used in this publication meets the minimum requirements of American National Standard for Information Sciences—Permanence of Paper for Printed Library Materials, ANSI/NISO Z39.48-1992.

Printed in the United States of America

In memory of the late Robert Barr Smith,
soldier, scholar, attorney, loyal friend,
and American patriot

CONTENTS

Introduction

Thirteen months before his death in early February 2013 at the hands of a severely troubled veteran he was helping, Chris Kyle became America's most famous sniper. His best-selling memoir, *American Sniper*, became a highly popular film in 2014.

The Greatest Navy SEAL Stories Ever Told, the most recent book in this series, launched in 2016 with my friend, coauthor, and military historian, the late Robert Barr Smith, included several lesser-known stories about Chris Kyle and a few other accomplished SEAL snipers.

The book that the reader now holds includes often overlooked stories of well-known contemporary American snipers but focuses primarily upon other practitioners of the silent art who few modern readers in this genre have experienced before.

Chronologically, these stories begin in the Iron Age and end so recently that the only reliable written sources at the time of writing were newspaper articles by well-respected, objective journalists reporting for the *Wall Street Journal*, the *New York Times*, and other top-shelf newspapers.

When multiple sources for this book were available, they were carefully reviewed and compared, with a distinct preference for carefully vetted memoirs favorably reviewed by knowledgeable, experienced, and widely recognized experts. Sources for the American Revolution, World War II, and other conflicts prior to 9/11 include eyewitness accounts and histories compiled in most cases by military historians. In some cases, quotations were modified for consistency with modern language and terms used elsewhere in the text.

We begin this search for largely unknown snipers in the dead silence of a Friday night in south central France, at the dawn of the thirteenth century.

CHAPTER ONE

The Silent Art: Hunters on the Loose

RICHARD PUT ON HIS HEADGEAR AND PICKED UP A CROSSBOW, looked quickly at the chain-mail body armor nearby, but decided it just took too long to put on for a quick walk around the castle to check on the men. He needed a bit of shooting practice during the evening quiet that Friday at a place called Chalus in south central France, just a few days after he ordered and began this siege. Minutes later, he stared up at the forty or so besieged defenders on the walls thirty feet above him, talking to his own men as he walked along. Soon he spotted a man with a cooking pan knocking away the occasional arrow sent up by Richard's men when they weren't laughing. Some even clapped as if listening to a joke, just before Richard felt the pain in his left shoulder near the neck and looked down to see the crossbow arrow (called a bolt) that caused it. The laughter came to an abrupt halt as at least a hundred fingers pointed toward the crossbowman hiding behind the high wall. His name was Peter.

A few days later, after Chalus Castle was captured, Richard sat up on his cot just long enough to meet the crossbowman responsible for all this pain, telling Peter to hold out his hand as everyone wondered what was about to happen. Richard handed him one hundred shillings, worth at least eight thousand dollars in modern money before telling the soldiers around them that Peter was to be released unharmed.

Eight days later, on Tuesday April 6, 1199, twelve days before Easter, surrounded by soldiers and clergy while nestled in the arms of his mother Eleanor, Richard died. Within hours, Richard's men tortured and then hanged Peter despite the dead man's wishes. After all, Peter had killed Richard I, the English king called Lionheart.

—⁓—

He is known by many names in many places. From ancient Britain during the Roman occupation to the vast emptiness of modern Afghanistan, from Limousin in south central France to Vietnam, the warrior we call sniper has been an ambivalent character in military history, admired by some, despised by others, but feared by all.

Ancient legends of snipers known in earlier times by other names abound. In one such story, the legendary painter and sculptor Leonardo da Vinci shouldered a rifle during the 1520 siege of Florence, adding sharpshooting to his vast artistic talents. More certainly, the lesser-known yet highly talented artist Benevento Cellini served Pope Clement VII as a sharpshooter during a siege of Rome seven years later. Cellini shouldered a heavy matchlock musket, most likely killing the Constable of Bourbon and also injuring Philibert of Chalon, the Prince of Orange, despite an intense, earth-clinging fog.

The term "sharpshooter," *scharfschutzen* in German, was first used in Holland and Germany. English *arquebusiers* used weapons remarkably similar to modern rifles by 1547. English officers most likely invented the term "sniper" in late eighteenth-century India; officer correspondence of that era often described a day's hunting excursion as "going out sniping." The snipe is a small quick game bird that employs a twisted, erratic difficult-to-track flight pattern.

Describing sharpshooters or marksmen as snipers originated in World War I newspaper accounts. Soon thereafter, military authorities frequently used the term to describe sharpshooters using rifles equipped with telescopic sights fired from concealed positions. Twenty-first-century newspaper articles have in recent years begun using the term as a synonym for murderer, raising the ire of many military practitioners of the silent art.

Modern snipers now sharpen skills that sixteenth-century practitioners like Cellini never even dreamed of, in training so rigorous that often a 3rd of the would-be snipers in any given class wash out. The skill set is complex and wide-ranging, including but not limited to camouflage, map reading, intelligence gathering, and survival. The most critical skill, of course, is precision shooting, often from cramped spaces after hours, if not days of ideally motionless surveillance, knowing that if captured or even spotted a quick or prolonged, tortured death will soon follow.

Long ago, a *New York Times* reporter commented on these dangers in a Civil War profile of snipers then called sharpshooters, noting that if captured, silent art practitioners faced certain execution, as had been the case during the American Revolution.

A US Marine tradition holds that the quatrefoil, a four-pointed decoration on the top of a warrant or commissioned Marine officer's dress and service caps, sometimes called "barracks covers," originated during the Revolutionary War so that enlisted Marine snipers high in the ship riggings of the time could distinguish Marine officers from enemy boarding parties. Modern experts note that the quatrefoil became official in 1859, not long after the American military began adopting French military styles.

During World War I, Australian infantryman George Mitchell diarized the frank admission that captured Turkish snipers were automatically bayoneted without exception at Gallipoli.

A Confederate sharpshooting duo working on Little Round Top during the Civil War Battle of Gettysburg fared better. After killing a colonel and several other senior Union officers, they escaped despite coming under extensive fire.

Through the ages, snipers have also often experienced hostility from their own comrades in the infantry, which makes one wonder why anyone would volunteer for, much less seek out, such duty. The chapters that follow answer that question and examine the experiences of highly skilled, little-known snipers.

Modern dictionary entries for snipers and sniping often include references to impression of ill will toward others and even at "someone shooting from a concealed position at unprotected people," a reference that would surprise many a lone wolf assigned to attack heavily armed enemies in large numbers, thereby risking immediate lethal retribution ranging from small arms fire to artillery and tanks to dive bomber runs.

Modern archeologists have established at least one instance of sniping by Roman soldiers. An ancient Briton skeleton extracted beneath Maiden Castle, an Iron Age fortification dating to 600 BC romanticized by Thomas Hardy and other nineteenth-century English writers, sports an iron bolt fired from a Roman ballista (bolt thrower) all but certainly shouldered by a Roman soldier.

Cellini at least has left us a description of his 1527 sniping experiences in Rome. He packed his matchlock musket with powder sufficient for shots at enemy soldiers some two hundred Roman paces, 322 yards away. This gave Cellini fighting advantages that his enemies could only dream about.

That said, modern snipers often play equally critical roles in modern warfare. During the 1982 Falklands war between the United Kingdom and Argentina, sniper fire was commonplace. This reality prompted a British soldier named Lukowiak to simply adopt an air of resignation after seeing one of his closest friends killed by a sniper in hiding.

"It was so close I felt it [the sniper attack] physically. All of us dived to the ground and crawled up to the hedge in search of cover," Lukowiak recalled. "Someone asked if anybody had spotted the enemy. Slowly, one by one, we began to look over the hedge. There was nothing there, just an open field and another empty field beyond that." Another shot seemed to fly by but Lukowiak's friend Tony fell to the ground screaming. Someone called out, "It's a fucking sniper."

That last comment during the Lukowiak experience reminds us of one fact that's not terribly obvious. Snipers historically have been disliked almost as much by their own infantry comrades as by enemy soldiers. The reason is logical, but disquieting. The presence of a sniper in the midst of or near other soldiers often brings enemy fire. During World War I, that enemy fire often came in the form of artillery shells or mortar rounds. Beyond this, most soldiers then shared a respect for human life, temporarily suspended in war yet sometimes broken by snipers who stalked the enemy as if that enemy were an animal being hunted.

These considerations combined to give World War I snipers the reputation of cold-blooded killers. One British sniping officer who served in France during World War I later confirmed that regular infantry soldiers didn't mix well with snipers. Another writer noted the tendency in the regular infantry to see snipers as unprincipled "hunters on the loose" with whom regular infantry soldiers seldom, if ever, socialized. Vietnam-era US Marine snipers frequently overheard themselves described as "Murder Incorporated."

Unlike regular World War II infantrymen, few snipers agreed to be interviewed by journalists or even pose for photographs before or during that conflict. They feared being singled out for deviating from traditional notions of "sporting warfare," namely the notion that killing adversaries from hiding is cowardly.

Henry Furness, a British World War II veteran whose specific rank had been sniper sergeant, offers a rare glimpse into this experience. After shooting a German officer during one mission, enemy artillerymen struck his position with such ferocity that Furness was knocked out of his foxhole—twice. A Furness letter later noted that snipers were individualistic, often solitary men who had the right outlook for that type of killing. Furness described them as frequently quiet and cautious loners, who drank only moderately and were usually nonsmokers, a rarity during World War II. Most snipers were exempt from normal frontline tasks such as guard duty. They usually worked in secret.

Native American John Fulcher and other snipers of that background sometimes heard other Americans call them savages. Even during the 1980s, one British sniper outfit was called the Leper Colony. We will also explore how this negativity snipers frequently heard from their own comrades impacted the sniper outlook and explore an equally critical question. How does one come to grips with that first killing from hiding?

World War I British sniper Charles Burridge was forever haunted by the first German he killed. That said, anecdotal evidence indicates that snipers with extensive prior experience in hunting for big game saw sniping as a form of trophy hunting. American John George, who took out numerous Japanese machine gun nests during World War II, at least had the consolation of seeing previously pinned-down comrades waive him their thanks with smiles on their faces.

British sniper Harry Furness had to step over his first kill, a young, handsome German corporal whose face he never forgot. American sniper Jim Gibbore never shook the anxieties he experienced in his first operations against Vietcong sentries, enemies though they were. His knees weakened, his hands shook, and breathing became difficult as he leaned into his scope, knowing that if the kill was not instantaneous, the target might awaken the entire Vietcong (VC) camp, which would likely then surround him. Fourteen dead VC later, Gibbore knew that he would be carrying that mission around for the rest of his life.

Post-9/11 American snipers faced these issues, and more, since technological advances in killing brought increased expectations of higher numbers and better results in difficult operating conditions. "Better stuff" enabled longer shots at more targets in less time than ever before. Beyond these dramatically increased expectations, snipers now work in more complex environments, often with fewer clear lines separating friends from enemies.

Thus, American snipers operating in Somalia during and after the Black Hawk Down era sometimes faced great uncertainties as to which warring factions were "friendly," the durability of such "friendships," and which factions were "friends" of the Americans at any given time.

Despite all this, dirty wars in Vietnam, Somalia, and elsewhere have increased career-building opportunities for snipers while also bringing them into increasingly dangerous environments as we shall see in the chapters that follow.

But before all that comes the American Revolution.

CHAPTER TWO

Murphy's Big Shot

GENERAL SIMON FRASER PACED HIS FAVORITE HORSE UP AND DOWN the line, sometimes behind and sometimes in front of his beloved men in red, urging the British forces forward even as some among them urged him to get out of the rebel line of fire. Later, when he lay dying, Simon told one visitor that he saw the very man who shot him.

The first two shots hit his horse without effect. One hit the crupper, the leather loop passing under his *horse's* tail and buckled to the saddle. A second bullet passed through the thick horse mane just inches from Simon's legs. "Would it not be prudent for you to retire from this place?" one of his aides asked. No sooner had Fraser said "My duty forbids me to fly from this place" than a bullet hit his stomach.

The American Revolution began two years earlier on Wednesday, April 19, 1775, with a famous single shot by a rifleman yet to be identified at a place called Lexington Green. Ralph Waldo Emerson called this "the shot heard round in the world" in his 1837 poem "Concord Hymn." Now, on October 7, 1777, in the eastern reaches of New York Colony, General John "Gentleman Johnny" Burgoyne had hoped to bring this pathetic American rebellion to a quick end. Simon had been his right-hand man until that shot rang out.

This was not the first British encounter with American sharpshooters. English Major George Hanger, himself an expert marksman, recalled nearly being killed by an American sharpshooter while patrolling with Lieutenant Banastre Colonel Tarleton. He observed a rifleman walk across a mill dam; lie down on his stomach; take cool and deliberate aim at Hanger, Tarleton, and their bugler; and then send a bullet through them, striking their bugler's horse. Hanger estimated the American marksman to be at least four hundred yards away. In a separate encounter at Fort Meigs on the Ohio River in present-day Perrysburg, Ohio, an unknown American shot a British allied Native American out of a tree from at least six hundred yards, or so the story goes.

The American Congress authorized Pennsylvania to recruit and enlist six companies of "long rifleman" in June 1775. Later, an additional three companies joined this compliment, now commanded by Daniel Morgan, himself an expert rifleman. Two decades earlier, Daniel Morgan developed sharpshooting techniques employed by American snipers to this day.

Decades earlier, American patriot Richard Henry Lee noted that six frontier counties of the Virginian Commonwealth could produce some six thousand Indian fighters who could travel with light provisions. These marksmen practiced shooting at targets no closer than two hundred yards away and no larger than an orange. Other observers of that time wrote that these frontiersmen could hit targets at a distance of 250 yards or ever farther.

Morgan's fighting philosophy for using long rifles was simple: kill the officers. And so, when came the American Revolution, he trained "Morgan's Sharpshooters" to shoot for the epaulets—flat, ornamental shoulder pieces once worn by officers of all armies.

This focus on killing British officers was a Morgan innovation, one that the British considered unsporting well into the twentieth century. Sporting or not, the strategy was highly effective and used by both sides.

In fact, according to one source, several years later, George Washington narrowly escaped a similar fate at the hands of one Patrick Ferguson, a Scotsman who had developed his own rifle. According to his own account, just before sustaining a wound at the Battle of Brandywine on September 11, 1777, Ferguson claimed that he saw an obviously important American officer accompanied by another man in unusual hussar (light infantry) dress, identified years later as Count Casimir Pulaski, described by some sources as the father of the American Cavalry. Ferguson learned from a surgeon that the potential target may have been General Washington but said that he had no regrets about deciding not to kill the man, whoever he was, since "Washington" was not facing him. Ferguson was later killed at the Battle of King's Mountain.

The shots fired on April 19, 1775, in Lexington eventually motivated the Continental Congress to summon ten companies of "expert rifleman," two from Virginia, another pair from Maryland, and six from Pennsylvania. The Frederick County, Virginia, men elected Morgan captain of their company.

Years later, Morgan's early recruits, including twenty-two-year-old Peter Bruin remembered how Morgan had many choices but took only the best marksman. Morgan's sharpshooters, ninety-six in number, about twenty-eight over his allotted number, typically wore Indian clothing and brought their own rifle, tomahawk and scalping knife.

Marching north some six hundred miles toward Cambridge, Massachusetts, Morgan's rifles, in a few instances, paid for their meals by putting on marksmanship shows. Arriving in Cambridge five days before any of the other Virginia companies made Morgan and his men instant local celebrities before they established their camp at Roxbury. Their first targets were British soldiers nearby on Boston Neck.

Morgan's men and the other sharpshooters targeted British sentries, stragglers, and the occasional British officer ambling through the area. In early September, Morgan and his company was selected for an expedition that was to push north through present-day Maine into Canada, under the command of a thirty-four-year-old former pharmacist from New Haven, Connecticut, Colonel Benedict Arnold. During the ill-fated Quebec campaign, Morgan was captured and offered a colonelcy in the British Army, which he refused.

Morgan and other paroled prisoners arrived at Elizabethtown, New Jersey, on September 24, 1776. Four days later, General Washington wrote to John Hancock, then serving as president of the Continental Congress, recommending that Captain Daniel Morgan become commanding officer of the rifle regiment. Washington believed that "in his [Morgan's] promotion, the States will gain a good and valuable officer for the sort of troops he is particularly recommended to command." Hancock responded a few days later that the rifle regiment Washington spoke of would be reserved for Morgan.

Late December 1776 brought Morgan his commission and appointment as colonel of the 11th Virginia Regiment. Following his formal prisoner exchange in January, Morgan covered most of western Virginia looking for the best sharpshooters he could find and marched to Washington's winter encampment in Morristown, New Jersey, with 180 men, far short of the six-hundred-man compliment he sought to recruit.

The spring 1777 campaign brought Morgan a special assignment from General Washington. Since the 11th Virginia was only at 30 percent of typical regimental strength, Washington tasked Morgan to command some five hundred troops from the western regions of Pennsylvania, Maryland, and Virginia armed with rifles and spikes in June 1777. This light infantry, formally named the Provisional Rifle Corps, dressed almost to a man in backwoods hunting shirts and leggings.

The sharpshooters were ordered north to assist the American Northern Army in the resistance against General "Gentleman Johnny" Burgoyne's drive south toward Albany, New York. By July 29, Burgoyne had already taken Fort Miller, fifty-eight miles south of Fort Ticonderoga and just north of a newly established village called Saratoga Springs.

Morgan's sharpshooters had gained something of a reputation by now. One New York legislator pined "for some Virginia riflemen." August 17 brought Morgan a letter from General Washington, directing Morgan's Provisional Rifle Corps to Peekskill, New York, where they would board boats for Albany and eventual battle with Native Americans loyal to British general Burgoyne. Washington's scheme was to use the sharpshooters to harass Burgoyne's Indians into wholesale desertions. And so, American major general Horatio Gates, the most unmilitary-looking general in military history, waited anxiously for the arrival of Morgan's sharpshooters on August 29 at the intersection of the Hudson and Mohawk rivers.

His opponent of the moment, "Gentleman Johnny Burgoyne," called Gates the "old midwife." Many Americans agreed with him. Small, ruddy, four-eyed, and silver-haired, Gates had turned fifty on July 26 but looked and acted much older.

Early September found Gates, Benedict Arnold, and Daniel Morgan reorganizing the growing American Northern Army, now seven thousand troops strong, in preparation for the battle with Burgoyne the American generals knew was coming. The only question was where and when.

Bemis Heights, a high plateau with deep ravines, now in the midst of autumn leaves, just sixteen miles from Gates's new camp at the mouth of the Mohawk, seemed to be the perfect place to take the high ground and wait for Burgoyne. Gates added another three hundred sharpshooters equipped with bayonets commanded by Major Henry Dearborn to Morgan's Provisional Rifle Corps. While Gates and Arnold's conventional forces began preparing fortifications, Morgan's sharpshooters began conducting reconnaissance operations against Burgoyne.

Late on the morning of September 19, Morgan's sharpshooters perched in the high treetops above Freeman's Farm spotted Burgoyne's army.

The Gates battle plan, as modified at the suggestion of Benedict Arnold, called for Morgan's sharpshooters to attack from behind trees in a heavily worded area north of the American camp, before the Redcoats could emerge onto clear ground.

Just after 1:00 p.m. that afternoon, Morgan's sharpshooters began sniping at Burgoyne's own 1,100 men, causing the redcoats to run for a sheltering pine grove to the north of Gates position. Soon the redcoats came back into the clearing, using their bayonets to force Morgan's men back into the foliage south of Freeman's Farm. Many of Morgan's sharpshooters climbed up into the tall trees. And from those hiding places, they picked off virtually all of the recoat artillerymen visible to their north. And even worse was ahead for the British.

Burgoyne directed that the British 21st Regiment on his right stretch out as much as possible to avoid being flanked. This left a gap in the middle of the battlefield, making the 62nd Regiment in the middle highly vulnerable with both of its flanks exposed to Morgan's sharpshooters. And exploit it they did. The 62nd Regiment comprised some six hundred men was decimated. Joseph Yeadon, a twenty-one-year-old drummer born in the town of Scarva, twenty-six miles southwest of Belfast, Northern Ireland, was one of the sixty 62nd Regiment survivors that day.

Morgan's sharpshooters, many of them invisible as a practical matter in the trees high above Freeman's Farm, had killed a large number of British officers, effectively leaving Burgoyne with no artillery, few officers at the company level. The survivors were saved only by the setting sun.

Despite these losses, Burgoyne resolved to fight his way to Albany rather than retreat. To that end, on Tuesday October 7, 1777, Burgoyne moved the 1,500 men or so under his immediate command to a point some four miles north of present-day Schuylerville, where he surveyed the ground in front of them, finding nothing, since Morgan's sharpshooters were hiding out of plain sight in the deep woods to their front and on their flanks.

Morgan had assumed that the day's battle would begin this way and had made a recommendation to Generals Gates and Benedict Arnold. Instead of following convention with a frontal attack, Morgan strongly suggested that he lead his forces through the foliage to a high hill position near the British right flank and strike just after American force commanded by Brigadier General Enoch Poor struck the British left flank. Gates approved Morgan's proposed plan of battle without a single change.

General Poor's division began the battle at 2 p.m. striking the British with such good effect that the Americans captured a cannon and promptly turned it on the British, just as Morgan's sharpshooters did something unusual, charging down a hill opening fire as they went, soon compelling the British light infantry led by Alexander

Lindsay, 6th Earl of Balcarres (Lord Balcarres), to retreat back into the British lines.

That accomplished, Morgan now focused on blue-uniformed Brunswick forces commanded by Major General Baron von Riedesel but was initially repelled. Morgan's second charge sent the outnumbered Brunswick Germans back toward their lines, at least until General Simon Fraser, riding a gray horse, brought up the British 24th Regiment and began riding back and forth behind them, trying to stop the retreat, at least until Morgan took action.

According to the traditionally told American version of events, at this point Morgan directed one of his best riflemen, Tim Murphy, to shoot and kill Fraser. Usually portrayed in prints of that era as a broad-shouldered, dark-furrowed frontiersman wearing a large coonskin hat, Murphy climbed a tall tree and targeted Fraser with a double-barreled rifle. Murphy mortally wounded Fraser with the 3rd shot. Or at least that's the version of events Morgan related years later to a British officer and recounted in an 1853 article in the Virginia History Register.

Supposedly, Fraser's last words to the young wife of Major General Baron von Riedesel were, "Oh fatal ambition! Poor General Burgoyne! My poor wife!" However Fraser's life ended, the Americans now had the opportunity to achieve victory that day. After Benedict Arnold spontaneously led some troops driving some Canadians and Native Americans out of the area, only a battalion of German mercenaries under the command of Lieutenant Colonel Heinrich von Breymann stood between the Americans and victory at Saratoga. Arnold and Morgan routed the last of the Germans, who sought refuge behind a redoubt, but Breymann was so furious that he bayoneted four of his own men, before one of the surviving Germans shot him.

Later, as Burgoyne with those few effective British forces remaining hurried north along the Hudson River, Gates dispatched several units to surround him. Ten days after the struggle at Bemis Heights, on Friday, October 17, 1777, Burgoyne surrendered at Saratoga.

Many of the British officers and enlisted men, including Joseph Yeadon, were marched to New York City and on to a prisoner of war camp at Charlottesville, Virginia. Yeadon was one of the Irish prisoners who joined the American Army. In 1781, the young Irishman participated in battles against British allied Shawnee Indians at present-day Louisville, Kentucky, alongside Thomas Norman, the grandfather of Edwin Stanton. Seventy-nine years later, Stanton served as secretary of war to President Abraham Lincoln. When Lincoln was assassinated, it was Edwin Stanton who said, "Now he belongs to the ages." After the American victory over the British, young Joseph Yeadon married Mary Pennypacker. During the battle of Germantown, Pennsylvania, General Washington and many of his soldiers stayed at Pennypacker Mills, her grandparent's home. Joseph and Mary Yeadon were this writer's fifth grandparents.

More importantly, despite the American loss at Germantown, Pennsylvania, on October 4, the rebel victory at Bemis Heights three days later persuaded the French to enter the war against Britain on the side of the Americans, thanks in no small part to an American sniper known as Tim Murphy.

CHAPTER THREE

Green Coats and Long Rifles

Exposed to a deadly and desultory fire, and rendered doubly conspicuous by his glaring red habiliment, the English soldier, in particular, has but little chance with the American rifleman who, conscious of his advantage, and taking deliberate aim, seldom fails to attain his object; while his adversary, I am persuaded, out of ten shots that he fires, discharges not three with effect . . . an English army in the woods may be considered as so many victims led forth to unavoidable and unprofitable slaughter.

—JOHN RICHARDSON,
Tecumseh, or the Warrior of the West (1828)

ONE EIGHTEENTH-CENTURY BRITISH OBSERVER OVERSTATED THE skills of American sharpshooters, but not by much, describing them as "unerring marksman, seeing a small red squirrel when a British soldier would not see an elephant; and therefore, in forest warfare a much more formidable foe than the Imperial Guard of France, whose fire at 400 yards would seldom hit a church." Yet another Englishman was even blunter, complaining that "British soldiers stand up in the field and open themselves up to their enemies and they despise an enemy that sulks behind a rock or tree. The American rifleman, sustained by his passive courage in a situation of danger, conveys the idea of an assassin waiting for his victim."

That said, many are surprised to learn that companies of riflemen disappeared from the national American army order of battle almost as soon as the British surrender at Yorktown marked the end of the revolution. This of course did not mean the end of the American marksmanship traditions or of the state militias that maintained them. General "Mad" Anthony Wayne staged a temporary sharpshooter revival of sorts eleven years later as part of his legion system, but the army discarded it almost as soon as warring Native Americans were defeated at the 1794 battle of Fallen Timbers near present-day Toledo, Ohio, according to John Fredericksen's book *Green Coats and Glory: United States Regiment of Riflemen*, the main source for much of this chapter.

This is not to say that the idea of making sharpshooters armed with long rifles a fundamental component of the American order of battle was totally abandoned. To the contrary, when John Adams, Washington's successor as president, asked Washington for his advice as to the composition of the American army, he opined that "a corps of riflemen will be for several purposes extremely useful." Not long thereafter, Congress explicitly authorized the president "at his discretion to organize, officer and raise a battalion of riflemen" in an Act promulgated on March 3, 1799, in preparation for the so-called "Quasi-War," a series of naval battles and skirmishes between France and the United States from early July 1798 until late September 1800. The impetus for raising a battalion of riflemen subsided with the Quasi-War, but three years later, Henry Dearborn, a Revolutionary War veteran with a deep love of things military, became secretary of war. He initiated the design and manufacture of a weapon with the advantages of the Kentucky long rifle but none of its perceived inadequacies.

The Dearborn initiative resulted in the Harper's Ferry Model 1803 Rifle, the first product manufactured by the US government, which soon became the weapon of choice for state militias, since it could throw a .54-caliber ball accurately through a .33-caliber barrel.

Five years later, Congress authorized a ten-company 680-enlisted-men rifle regiment to be commanded by a colonel. The ten companies were to be dispersed along the frontier, each company lead by a captain, with appropriate compliments of lieutenants, sergeants, corporals, and two musicians for good measure. Two companies were recruited from the more remote regions of New York and Vermont, but most the riflemen came from the Louisiana and Mississippi Territories as well as Kentucky, Ohio, and the Indiana Territory. Supply depots were located at Shepardstown, (West) Virginia, and Savannah, Georgia.

Unlike the regular troops, these riflemen wore green coats; green pantaloons; a tall, cylindrical military cap with a visor called a shako; green plumes; and yellow tassels. Alexander Smyth (not Smith) of Virginia was the first colonel. He was a skilled politician and a lawyer with no military experience whatsoever. Smyth was a marginal performer but did well enough to eventually become inspector general of the army in July 1812, only to be cashiered for incompetence.

The year before, in early November, a rifle regiment company commanded by Captain Moses Whitney then stationed in Newport, Rhode Island, joined the 4th US Infantry near Philadelphia. Soon the US Army combined force rendezvoused with an expedition led by Indiana governor William Henry Harrison. The expedition marched on to Tippecanoe, Indiana Territory, on the site of present-day Battleground, Indiana, some 5.6 miles northwest of Prophetstown. The governor sought to parlay with and if necessary engage the Shawnee and several allied tribes that opposed US expansion into their lands.

Early the next morning, a combined force of Indians staged a surprise attack, during which the US Riflemen Company held its position despite heavy fire from the Indians and the loss of the Private Ira Trowbridge, earning the praise of Governor Harrison, who, partially upon the reputation earned in this battle, was elected president of the United States in 1840.

Four months later, on St. Patrick's Day, 1812, citizens of Georgia squatting in Spanish Florida began the so-called Patriot War by seizing Amelia Island off the Florida coast. They were soon joined by Lieutenant Colonel Thomas A. Smith leading two rifle companies composed of one hundred badly armed and poorly equipped men sent without proper supplies to defend the Georgia squatters against a possible British intervention. The next month he pushed into the mainland, beginning at St. Augustine, the capital of Spanish East Florida, drawing the ire of Governor Sebastian Kindelan. The military and political "engagements" that followed had the makings of a tragic yet comic opera.

Commanding a weak and vulnerable force at best, Lieutenant Colonel Smith stared at the high imposing walls of Castillo de San Marcos, which he justifiably described as "one of the strongest fortified places on the continent, containing a garrison five times our number." He wondered out loud what he was supposed to do. Modest reinforcements provided by Governor Kindelan arrived to share in the continuing deprivation made worse by Seminole attacks on the already scarce supply trains. Having succeeded his predecessor Alexander Smyth, a gray-headed, sharp-beaked gentlemen as the full colonel in command on July 6, 1812, three months later, Smith moved his forces to the St. Johns River near the Georgia border and, after more hardships, was ordered north in March 1813 to join the Army of the Northwest, a unit of the US Army that had been formed at the outset of the War of 1812 the preceding June, bringing the "Patriot War" debacle to an end.

Benjamin Forsyth, a North Carolina native who commanded a rifle regiment company during that war developed a reputation for plunder and raiding that some historians have described as fully justified. Just after the War of 1812 commenced, Forsyth led his company from New York City to Sackets Harbor some 315 miles to the north, arriving in late July. Two months later, in mid-September, the district military commander authorized a raid on Gananoque, a French Canadian village some forty miles further north. Forsyth ordered his seventy riflemen and some thirty militias into boats on September 18 arriving in the village in time to surprise a detachment of the Leeds Militia three mornings later, killing ten, capturing eight, and torching all the supplies the riflemen could not carry.

Several weeks later, Forsyth received a politically delicate assignment at Ogdensburg, New York, a federalist outpost seventy miles north of Sackets Harbor, many of whose merchants were suspected

British sympathizers. From Ogdensburg, Forsyth could see Prescott, a Canadian town on the other side of the St. Lawrence River, guarded by plump, well-dressed British soldiers. This was in sharp contrast with Forsyth's own poorly dressed troops, who Forsyth claimed were almost naked.

US Army leadership promoted Captain Forsyth to major in mid-January 1813, and another opportunity to distinguish himself emerged in early February. Several Americans had been kidnapped and jailed in Elizabethtown, Upper Canada, present-day Brockville, Ontario. Forsyth put together a two-hundred strong force consisting of his own company and several militias and then proceeded by sleigh ride from Ogdensburg to Morristown, New York, twelve miles upstream on the St. Lawrence, nearly opposite Elizabethtown. Crossing the St. Lawrence at three the next morning, Forsyth personally led his men storming the jail, freed sixteen Americans, and captured forty-six privates, two lieutenants, and the commanding major of the unlucky 1st Leeds Militia, whose record against Forsyth was now zero for two. Not only that, Forsyth recovered 120 stands of arms the British took from American forces at Detroit, earning for this mission a brevet promotion to lieutenant colonel made retroactive to February 6.

Now known as "a terror to the enemy," Forsyth now entertained Lieutenant Colonel "Red George" MacDonnell of the Glengarry Light Infantry "Fencibles," an antiquated term referencing troops raised strictly for defense purposes. Red George claimed during a visit to Ogdensburg under a flag of truce that American troops in the area were stealing private property, just before Forsyth abruptly wished him a good evening.

Little wonder then that Lieutenant Colonel MacDonnell returned to Ogdensburg early on the morning of February 22 with at least eight hundred men, quickly scattering the American militias before charging Forsyth's company of riflemen ensconced in an old stone fort. Forsyth refused to surrender but slipped away to Black Lake, some sixteen miles to the south, leaving the Americans in Ogdensburg undefended. From the comparative safety of Black Lake, Forsyth urgently requested more troops, promising his commander, Colonel Alexander

Macomb, that he would retake Ogdensburg and Prescott, an Upper Canada town just across the St. Lawrence from it.

Although the Forsyth request was denied, he invented a new sharpshooting technique two months later during an April 27, 1813, attack on York in Upper Canada, under the command of General Zebulon M. Pike, who seven years earlier in 1806 attempted to climb the famous Colorado peak eventually named for him.

Now, on April 27 after having his buglers sound charge for a conventional face-to-face attack, Forsyth had his men take cover and fire at will at a company of grenadiers who were decimated charging Forsyth's men head on. One surviving grenadier of the 8th (King's) Regiment told an acquaintance that he had never seen anything like it. A second Forsyth-ordered bugle call a few minutes later scattered British-allied Indians in all directions.

York now fell into American hands but at a cost. General Pike was mortally wounded and scores of casualties inflicted by an exploding magazine deliberately set by the fleeing redcoats just before the riflemen and other Americans pillaged the town.

Fort George, at the mouth of the Niagara River was the next American target in late May, with Forsyth's 1st US Rifle Regiment leading the way in as the vanguard. George McFeely of the 22nd Infantry later recounted his experience with one of Forsyth's sharpshooters, a man named Shoops: "When some of our men (the 22nd Infantry) were firing into the air at an angle of forty-five degrees, others in their confusion did not ram the cartridge [even] half-way home, dropped their ramrods on the ground and indeed some rendered their muskets useless in the fight by firing away their rammers [ram rods]." He remembered that Shoops somehow "remained cool and collected, he lowered his rifle and took his aim as deliberately as if he had been shooting at a mark . . . I have no doubt that every ball fired by this brave fellow took effect as the range was only forty yards."

That said, the rifle regiment company pillaged the town as it had done at York, some even strutting about in English officer uniforms they found in a deserted British barracks. An American sailor later said of the rifle regiment that "one was never safe with them on the field of battle, friend or foe." Another observer worried about allowing the rifle company to pull guard duty later in the campaign at a place called Stoney Creek on June 6, noting that "they had never been disciplined to picket-duty, and would therefore probably, wherever they might be stationed, lie down and go to sleep."

Soon thereafter Van Swearingen's Rifle Company, assigned to guard duty near a church in Stoney Creek, went to sleep inside and was captured, along with both American generals on the operation.

Despite these shortcomings, when the rest of the Americans fell back to the Fort George vicinity, Forsyth and his remaining sharpshooters, augmented by some two hundred Seneca Indians loyal to the American cause, surprised a party of British-allied Indians. This small success set the stage for large-scale sharpshooter responsibilities during the fall 1813 Montreal expedition led by American general James Wilkinson. That November, several detachments of sharpshooters led by Forsyth but commanded by Colonel Alexander Macomb struggled upstream against the St. Lawrence River current, clearing out pockets of Canadians as they progressed. November 7 found Forsyth storming ashore to face enemy guns.

Four days later, downstream at a place called Hoople's Creek near present-day Cornwall, Ontario, Forsyth's rifles held their own once again in an engagement with a sizable Canadian force. A letter from Captain Rufus McIntire noted one particular act of valor by Ensign James of the Rifle corps who pursued some six or eight of the Canadians by himself, killing one and taking another captive.

Wilkinson's expedition suffered a severe loss that very Thursday, November 11, in a battle at Crysler's (not Chrysler's) farm in which vastly outnumbered British and Canadian forces repelled the Americans. Consequently, an American council of war held the next day decided to discontinue the Montreal expedition.

This debacle didn't reflect badly on Forsyth or his sharpshooters. "Your rifle boys are fine, active useful fellows, Colonel Edmund P. Gaines," who six years earlier had arrested Aaron Burr on behalf of the US government but now served as adjutant of the 25th Infantry

Regiment, wrote Colonel Smith, going on to say that "I wish you were here with them and had 20, instead of your present number of companies."

Whether or not by pure coincidence, the US government shared the Gaines sentiment. Several months after the disaster at Crysler's farm, Congress augmented the rifles on February 10, 1814, in an act calling for three additional regiments for five years' service unless the war ended earlier.

Even before those additional rifle regiments were formed, tragedy struck 1st Regiment sharpshooters recuperating from their injuries. British and Indian forces burning Buffalo, New York, in January 1814, reputedly murdered several riflemen in hospital. Undeterred by this, Forsyth led 1st Rifle Regiment forces against elements of the Canadian Frontier Light Infantry during the last Canadian invasion led by the increasingly desperate General James Wilkinson, following the failure of his Montreal expedition. This time Wilkinson directed troops wintering at French Mills, present-day Fort Covington, New York, to attack La Colle Mill, sixty-eight miles to the east just over the Canadian border.

Once again, Forsyth led his 1st Rifle Regiment sharpshooters into action, this time as the vanguard of American troops attacking the British 13th Regiment supported by part of the Canadian Frontier Light Infantry. Two sharpshooters were quickly lost, before the British forces retreated into the three-story mill now serving as a makeshift fort. There, the redcoats inflicted some two hundred casualties upon the Americans before Wilkinson terminated the attack and sulked back to French Mills, knowing that his removal as American commander of the troops in the St. Lawrence River Theater of war was only a matter of time.

Six months later, on June 28, at Odelltown, Quebec, just three miles south of La Colle Mill, Forsyth ran out of luck while operating yet another ambush against some seven or eight hundred British forces. Forsyth disregarded orders to fall back as quickly as the trap was sprung but instead stood his ground and was mortally wounded, telling his troops to "Rush on," with his last breath.

One month and thirteen days later, Forsyth's riflemen exacted revenge under the command of Lieutenant Bennett Riley, mortally wounding a captain of the Canadian Frontier Light Infantry near Odelltown. Some of the heaviest fighting of the war took place in the Niagara River area that summer, and the US Rifle regiment was often in the thick of it.

Little-known Ludowick Morgan, a major from Maryland, played an instrumental role in the battle for Buffalo in early August 1814. He sensed British movements along the Niagara River and speculated that the redcoats might be planning to attack Buffalo, after feigning an attack on Fort Niagara, some thirty-two miles north of Buffalo on Lake Ontario. Morgan posted all 240 riflemen under his command below Conjockta Creek, just north of Buffalo. After raising a breastwork and partially dismantling a bridge, Morgan and his men made a noisy march back to Buffalo, but only temporarily.

Suspecting that the British were up to something, he quietly led his troops back to the breastworks they built just hours before and waited for the British. The redcoats did not disappoint. Just after midnight on Wednesday, August 3, 1814, some six hundred light troops (riflemen) led by Lieutenant Colonel John Tucker crossed the Niagara, reaching the bridge that the Americans just partially dismantled at Conjockta Creek. Major Jonathan Kearsley, commander of the 4th US Rifle Regiment, recalled, "No sooner had the [British] platoon reached the bridge for the purpose of its repair than the signal from Major Morgan's whistle produce a discharge, deliberate and unerring from every [American] rifle. The British column, as far as it had advanced to the height of the ground or beyond it to the creek, was literally decapitated, not a man in view standing."

The panicked British blundered back to a nearby tree line and started sporadically exchanging shots with the Americans. A Private Byfield later remembered seeing one of the enemy daring enough to get up to the British breastworks immediately fall, not to rise again.

Undeterred, British lieutenant colonel Tucker ordered yet another advance, but when he did, Morgan's rifles killed every redcoat who came near the bridge.

Maryland's own Major Ludowick Morgan remembered what happened next: "They [the British] then attempted to flank up by sending a large body up the creek to ford it, when I detached Lieutenants Ryan, Smith and Armstrong, with about 60 men to oppose their left wing, where they were again repulsed with considerable loss."

Tucker called off the entire mission and retreated with his remaining forces to Canada. Although in modern terms Conjockta Creek is considered a skirmish rather than a battle, the implications were immense. One historian described it as the sharpshooter's finest hour during the War of 1812. "Had Tucker seized Buffalo [New York] and its supplies, the American garrison at Fort Erie would have been starved into submission and British forces could then ravage western New York, Erie or Detroit at their leisure. Morgan's victory forced Lieutenant General Sir Gordon Drummond to undertake a siege for which he was woefully unprepared. On this basis alone, Conjockta Creek must be ranked as a decisive defensive engagement of the war of 1812 and a clear strategic triumph for the United States." Kearsley, an eyewitness to the battle, described the role of the American sharpshooters the best: The skill in planning and the firmness in the execution by the riflemen defeated the designs of the British and saved the entire American army.

Sharpshooters fought sharpshooters once again a few days later when Morgan and his command crossed the Niagara River to Fort Erie for yet another duel of sorts with the Glengarry Fencibles, one of the many regiments of British light troops. This time, the battle went on for about two months. Lieutenant William Armstrong later regretted that lack of aggressiveness on the part of the commanding general kept his sharpshooters from finishing the job. "Had it not been for the general's caution not to pursue them [the British] too far, could have driven them into their camp. Our loss in killed and wounded is eighteen that of the enemy must have been far greater for after the action they were seen bringing up thirty-five men in blankets and it is said that the officer of the day was wounded." Armstrong bragged three days later that he "had the pleasure of seeing two of his Majesty's subjects fall by my own hand. I have had my share in five [skirmishes] and am as yet unhurt, but can't vouch how long it may be the case for we have been skirmishing almost every day."

That said, Ludowick Morgan, called "the Hero of Conjockta," fell at the hands of a British sharpshooter on Saturday, August 13, 1814, during a "heavy exchange." The details of his death provide insight into the raging battle. "A rifle or musket ball, shot obliquely from the left struck him in the left temple and passed through his head." Kearsley wrote telling his reader that "he [Morgan] fell instantly dead, leaving no more gallant soldier his survivor." The 1st and 4th US Rifles lost 20 percent of their strength during the month that followed.

British colonel William Drummond, no doubt bitter about his earlier losses, somehow got into Fort Erie, drawing the immediate attention of a company of American reinforcements from the 4th US Rifles commanded by Captain Benjamin Birdsall who later recalled what happened next: "I discovered a great number of troops," he recalled. "It being somewhat dark, I could not tell if they were British or American. I hailed them and [they answered] the 103rd. Being cautious to make no mistake, I was a second time answered 103rd after hailing a second time. Then I immediately ordered my men to fire."

Birdsall was severely wounded in the battle that followed, but this all ended when a magazine inside the fort exploded, killing most of the British. Official records show that by this time, the British siege of Fort Erie had cost 904 British casualties, both dead and wounded, as contrasted with 84 American casualties.

Despite these numbers, British colonel Drummond dragged the siege doubling down on his losses. The siege continued on through later August, when a British sortie killed and wounded a number of American officers. Tragic as this was for the patriots, the British experienced comparable damage when some of Wellington's forces laughed off the idea that they should not fight in the open against the Americans. The 82nd Regiment of Foot lost two killed and fifteen wounded in a matter of minutes by ignoring that advice on August 26.

Two hundred sharpshooters supported a September 17 attack against British lines, in which Colonel James Gibson, commander of the 4th US Rifle Regiment, fell. Lieutenant Lewis G. A. Armistead, whose older brother George commanded Fort McHenry in Baltimore Harbor when Francis Scott Key wrote the Star Spangled Banner, fell mortally wounded that day. The American counterattack at Fort Erie persuaded British commander William Drummond to withdraw.

Meanwhile, Tory governor general Sir George Prevost and some eleven thousand British veterans marched down the Champlain Valley toward Plattsburg, New York, some 676 miles northeast of Fort Erie, encountering the 29th US Infantry and some one hundred sharpshooters commanded by Lieutenant Colonel Daniel Appling on September 6. Prevost's massive forces, lumbered down Beekmantown Road toward their objective in Plattsburg, hounded all the way by the American sharpshooters, setting the stage for an attack from the woods adjacent to the road. One American sharpshooter later described the tactics that foretold what happened that day: "We had every opportunity of lying behind fences and secreting [*sic*] in the woods until they would arrive within gun [range], when we would fire and retire about half a mile." Using these sharpshooting tactics, the Americans inflicted some two hundred casualties on the British, Brevet Lieutenant Colonel Willington among them, while sustaining fifty-five casualties themselves.

Whether reluctant because of these losses or otherwise, Prevost didn't begin his attack on Plattsburg until September 11, giving the determined Americans all the time they needed to organize a fierce, determined defense that repulsed every British initiative, notably including the defense of the upper bridge on the Saranac River.

So, deterred and delayed, the Tory general turned tail and ran for Canada after learning that a British fleet had been destroyed on Lake Champlain, with American sharpshooters and infantry chasing them along the way. The green coats faced the prospect of taking scores and scores of English prisoners until Daniel Appling called off the pursuit due to the weather. "Soon after it commenced raining [Appling] ordered a countermarch and we returned to Plattsburg, thereby losing the finest opportunity of acquiring military distinction that had occurred. I regretted the circumstance for I had anticipated the taking of many prisoners," Major John E. Wool groused. Fainthearted or not, Appling soon received a brevet appointment to colonel.

Although the war in the Champlain Valley region was winding down, the sharpshooters of the US Regiment of Rifles operating in the region still found a few places to fight with distinction, notably at a little known place called Cook's Mills, Upper Canada, in present-day Welland, Ontario. British general Gordon Drummond gave up on taking Fort Erie on September 21, then moved to a makeshift defensive position called Fort Chippewa (Chippawa) on the north bank of Chippewa Creek sixteen miles north of Fort Erie.

American general James Izard and sharpshooters of the US Regiment of Rifles under his command marched from Plattsburg to reinforce Major General Jacob Brown and his men at Fort Erie but declined to pursue Drummond as Brown suggested, at least initially. Soon after, General Brown whisked his part of the army back to Sackets Harbor, leaving Izard an important decision to make by himself.

Finally, in mid-October, Izard moved his three-thousand-man force north to Chippewa Creek from Plattsburg, only to find the bridge over the impassable creek destroyed. Left with few options, Izard directed General Daniel Bissell and his nine-hundred-man brigade to Cook's Mill. On October 20, 750 British commanded by Lieutenant Colonel Myers attacked them but were suppressed by combined light troops and sharpshooters, who soon flanked the British. Ensign Elias Spurr became the last officer of the US Regiment of Rifles to die in the War of 1812.

Even as sharpshooters in northern New York celebrated the arrival of 1815 and began to wonder what they were going to do in peacetime, the last action of the 1st Regiment of Rifles occurred one thousand miles south of Buffalo at Fort Point Peter (identified in some sources as Point Petre) near present-day St. Mary's Georgia.

Company commander Captain Abram A. Massias of the 1st Regiment of Rifles learned on Tuesday, January 10, that a British force seemed to be headed in his direction.

Admiral Sir George Cockburn had landed on Cumberland Island off the Georgia coast, some eleven miles to the northeast. Cockburn's forces included three Royal Marine battalions, two companies from the 2nd West India Regiment, and assorted land forces consisting of at least 750 men.

With few choices and even fewer troops at his command, Massias left some thirty-six men at Fort Point Peter with instructions to destroy all the guns and promptly retire when the job was done. In the meantime, Massias placed his remaining combined force of soldiers and sharpshooters on either side of a narrow pass nearby.

Three days later on January 13, the British bombarded Fort Point Peter and then landed at nearby Point Peter, as Massias watched. When a combined force of some seven hundred sailors, marines, and soldiers from the 2nd West India Regiment approached the fort through the narrow passage silently surrounded by outnumbered American forces, Massias waited until the time was right and then opened fire but in the end retreated in the last engagement fought by the sharpshooters of the US Regiment of Rifles.

No one was surprised when the regiments were downsized from four units to one, commanded by Colonel Thomas A. Smith and headquartered in St. Louis. From there, the regiment of sharpshooters helped establish forts at Green Bay and Fort Smith, the first military installation of the Old Southwest, named for rifle regiment commanding officer Thomas A. Smith. Elements of the regiment participated in the 1819 Yellowstone Expedition. The sharpshooters among them included the once famous marksman Martin Scott.

Scott was born in Bennington, Vermont, twelve years after the United States declared its independence from England. His father Phineas was one of Bennington's earliest settlers. His education was meager, but Scott's skill as a sharpshooter became legendary. Among other skills, he could supposedly drive nails into wood with bullets and kill animals with headshots before sighting scopes were thought of, much less invented. Other undocumented sources claim that he killed his first bear at age twelve. A raccoon once surrendered to him to save his own life.

Raccoon rescuer or not, Scott was commissioned a 2nd Lieutenant in the 26th Infantry in April 1814 but was promoted to 1st Lieutenant less than a month later. Three years after his 1815 discharge from the US Army, he reenlisted in the Regiment of Rifles as a 2nd Lieutenant and was once again promoted to 1st Lieutenant, seventeen months later in June 1821. Within seven years, he had become a captain and represented the US Army at the Treaty of St. Peters between the United States and the Ojibwa tribes whereby lands in Minnesota and Wisconsin were ceded. One observer at Fort Mackinac described Scott as "an interesting man with strong alert, athletic figure, bright eager, keen grey eyes and ruddy face, bronzed by long exposure." The observer noted that he was a strong disciplinarian. The fort [he commanded] "was clean and orderly in the extreme." Even today, his photograph in the collection of the Bennington Museum in Vermont confirms all that and more.

He married a Miss McCracken of Rochester, New York, always kept good horses, a pack of hunting dogs, and the staff to take care of them. His reputation as a marksman only grew, one long tale claiming that Scott could throw two potatoes in the air and put a bullet through them with one shot. On the other hand, his fellow officers considered him antisocial, since he didn't drink or gamble. His tightfisted attitude about money not spent on rifles and hunting dogs probably stemmed from the fact that he supported both his mother and a sister back in Vermont. That said, his fellow officers constantly taunted him. One day he announced that he would shoot the next person who insulted him in a duel. Supposedly, a fellow officer named Keith took the challenge and shot Scott through the bowels, sustaining a chest wound himself, or so the story goes.

The war with Mexico brought him glory, promotion, and ultimately a hero's death. Bravery above and beyond duty brought him a brevet promotion to major after the battles of Palo Alto and Resaca de la Palma. Yet another battle brought yet another brevet promotion, this time to lieutenant colonel after the Battle of Monterey in early September 1846. Within a year he was dead, knocked off his horse at Molina Del Ray by a bullet through the heart. The next year Fort Martin Scott at Fredericksburg Texas was named for him.

The end came for the Regiment of Rifles scarcely two years later. When Secretary of War John C. Calhoun pressed future commanding general of the army Jacob Brown for suggested budget cuts, career-minded Brown succinctly targeted the sharpshooters: "If further reductions should be determined upon [*sic*] I would propose a derangement of the Rifle Regiment by transferring the rank and file to other corps. Riflemen, though deriving in actual service a high degree of importance from the nature of our country, I do not consider a *positively* essential arm of the peace establishment."

Congress voted the Regiment of Riflemen out of existence on March 2, 1821, but the organization and sharpshooter exploits were hardly forgotten. Sixteen years later, Major Bennet (not Bennett) C. Riley, who later served as the last military governor of California, wrote, "It is my opinion that a rifle regiment should be added to the peace establishment, as two wars have shown us that riflemen are the most efficient troops that were ever deployed by our country. Where can you find troops more efficient than Morgan's Riflemen of the Revolution or Forsyth's riflemen of the last war with Great Britain?" Riley recalled that he "served in Forsyth's riflemen during the whole of the last war, up to the reduction of the army in 1921, and have been in the infantry since, and have had a good opportunity of judging these two arms of service, and am decidedly of the opinion that the rifle [arm of service] is the best one the service can have."

An anonymous editorialist wrote the *Army and Navy Chronicle* in 1841, insisting "two rifle regiments might be advantageously engaged in perpetuating the skill in arms for which our soldiers have been so noted in the war of our revolution and in wars of subsequent date."

While this lesson was lost, however temporarily on the US authorities, the British consolidated their accomplished and widely recognized the 60th and 85th Regiments into a permanent standing Rifle Brigade.

One military historian claims that the Regiment of Riflemen was the most effective infantry formation fielded by the United States during the War of 1812, despite the debacle at Point Peter prompted by the extreme disparity between American and British forces. The scholar observed that "as Sandy Creek and Conjockta Creek amply demonstrate, the Regiment of Riflemen possessed tactical proclivities equal to any European army. They remain proud purveyors of the American Rifle tradition and one of the few bright spots in an otherwise dark period of US Army history."

Incidental ad hoc formations, such as the Voltigeurs of the Mexican War and a small Regiment of Mounted Riflemen, reflected the only organized sharpshooter presence in the American army until the formation of the 1st and 2nd US Sharpshooters under the command of Hiram Berdan at the beginning of the Civil War. And as we shall see, the Confederate Army had sharpshooters of its own.

CHAPTER FOUR

Blood for Blood

His own part of the Tennessee River lay some two hundred feet beneath him in the morning stillness, soon to be disturbed by the noise from yet another Yankee steamboat heading north downstream, that's right downstream toward old Paducah, Kentucky, or upstream going south away from that town of 4,600 occupied by the Yankees who now used it for a Federal supply depot.

The old man with the sharp features, oversized hat, and tan scarf could see everything for miles from this vantage point, a dense forest behind him to the east, to his right, the mouth of Leatherwood Creek that the boats had to pass churning upstream southward away from Paducah or in the opposite direction, past cornfields, and trees of all kinds, most anything a sniper would want to hide behind doing a day's work killing as many Yankee officers as possible. There was even bamboo here, perfect in better times for fishing poles to while away the hours.

He even had two islands to daydream about, Hurricane Island across the Tennessee and little Towhead Island, on Jack's side of the river, near the thing that brought him here, the Towhead Chute, a narrow, hazardous passage that river pilots had to slow down for. The entire Yankee flotilla had to come through here; there was no way around it. Transports full of Yankee troops, supply boats with food, and assorted gunboats all made their way past this point, if they could.

This was no easy task. The northbound trip was no fun, requiring pilots to be ever attentive during the rapid rush through the towhead run with high hopes and fingers crossed during the dangerous narrow run. The southbound boats slowly churned their way upstream a yard at a time, stuck in the Towhead Chute for as long as an hour, sometimes under the close scrutiny of rebel sharpshooters. And when the Yankees were very unlucky, Old Jack Hinson was one of the men peering down the barrel of a long rifle, hoping for a clear clean shot.

Jack had a special spot about twenty feet below the top of the bluff, practically invisible to the Yankees on the river yet close enough to take advantage of the sitting ducks dumb enough to hang around on the outside decks of supply boats struggling against the current past Towhead Chute.

Most mornings brought a steamboat or two full of Yankees who had no choice but to travel on the Tennessee River, with little or no warning that highly skilled sharpshooters like Jack Hinson were waiting to kill them.

This sunrise brought yet another steamboat that would pass just where Old Jack was expecting, mainly because there was no other option. Most mornings, Jack even had time to smoke a pipe while he watched and waited for just the right moment to shoot a Yankee. And if this pleasant morning went right, he might get a chance to kill two, three, or even more. It was all a matter of luck.

Jack Hinson was no spring chicken. At age fifty-seven, he had already exceeded the average life expectancy for American men in that era by eight years. Yet, he was tough and quick with extraordinary vision. Men he knew now called him "Captain Jack" rather than Old Jack. He lived in the "Between the Rivers" region marked by forested hills, cypress bays, cane breaks, and willow thickets where the Tennessee and Cumberland Rivers flowed within a few miles of each other in the northwestern corner of Middle Tennessee and Western Kentucky. The "Between the Rivers" region runs from north to south, more or less across five counties. Before the modern impoundment of lakes by the Tennessee Valley Authority, the people here relied on the rivers, swamps, and marshes for fish, other food sources, and transportation of their crops and goods to markets in Paducah and elsewhere. Many had come here directly or indirectly from Scotland or Northern Ireland, bringing a fierce independence, clannishness, and suspicion of "outsiders" observable to this day as far west as Oklahoma among their descendants. Unlike similar clans in Appalachia and the Ozarks, they were mountaineers without mountains but shared the same focus on purely local affairs and an often extreme indifference to the rest of the world.

Jack Hinson knew important people in his region. And among his closest friends was John Bell, former Speaker of the US House of Representatives and secretary of war under President Benjamin Harrison, according to his principal modern biographer, Tom C. McKenney (not McKinney), whose book *Jack Hinson's One-Man War* is the primary source for this chapter.

Stewart County, Tennessee, where Jack Hinson lived, raised and organized the 14th Tennessee Infantry Regiment during the early spring of 1861 with two adjoining counties. Nearby in Beverly, Kentucky, a Confederate company was raised in a single day for battles and hardships that most of the newly enlisted men could scarcely imagine.

Despite Jack Hinson's opposition to secession, his youngest son William soon rode into Dover, population 296, the Stewart County in Tennessee, to be sworn into the 14th Infantry Regiment by Brigadier General Daniel S. Donelson. William and the rest of the 14th Regiment soon boarded an express train for Virginia, arriving too late to fight in the July 2 skirmish known as the First Battle of Bull Run near Manassas, Virginia, but fought in thirty-three others. Jack and his wife Elisabeth heard nothing from or about William during July and August.

That fall, Union gunboats began appearing on the Cumberland and Tennessee Rivers, sometimes conducting raiding parties onshore in Kentucky. One Confederate officer sent to Fort Donelson remarked in his person journal that "the people in the counties of Trigg and Lyon Kentucky are calling on us every day for protection, and I think we are losing ground in that region simply because they are overawed by gunboats and small parties that come out from Smithland and steal everything that they can lay their hands upon."

Jack had wanted nothing to do with the war, but a tragedy had changed all that. Now Old Jack watched with his oversized rifle barrel resting on a tree branch as the gunboat he was targeting slipped into place for a forty-five-minute southbound trip up the Tennessee fighting a strong current. As the boat came ever closer, he began looking for the telltale shoulder pieces called epaulets of an officer unwittingly volunteering for a quick trip to the next world by showing himself on deck. Finally Hinson spotted one, leaning over the rail smoking a pipe as casually as he might on a day at the park.

Within seconds the earth collapsed to encompass just two men, the union officer, who seemed to be calling to the custom-made .50-caliber Kentucky rifle, and Old Jack, who rested on the barrel stock and waited for the slight breeze whispering in his ear to go silent. During the quiet that followed, Jack made his adjustments, relaxed, held his breath, and touched the trigger without squeezing it, as the officer fell backward on the boat deck. All the sailors around him began to dive for cover as the officer's legs twitched, but only momentarily. Eventually, a few of them aimed a deck gun or two at real or imagined whiffs of white smoke rising above ridge behind Old Jack. Neither the deck guns nor the small arms that some of the sailors fired even came close to the sharpshooter, who watched the medical men going through the motions of treating the dead naval officer. Old Jack's kill list exempted such men, placing a priority on officers, although he was not above killing an enlisted Yankee when his options were few.

Old Jack relaxed as the sailors went back to their regular duties, guiding the gunboat out into the main river channel once they passed the south end of Towhead Chute. Sitting quietly in the silence, he knew that the day's hunting was over. There was no smoke on the northern horizon, no shrill boat whistles, or any other sign that more Yankees were ready to die on the working end of his rifle that morning. He slowly and carefully cleaned his rifle, maybe even burnishing the small circles he had carved in the barrel of his rifle for each Yankee he had killed. Jack had to climb out of this hidey-hole one tree at a time, using his one free hand to pull himself from tree to tree ever upward, while carefully holding his Kentucky rifle in the other hand.

Even then, as Old Jack reached the top of the bluff, the Union surgeon looking down at his fellow officer could do little more than get him ready for burial. The enlisted men scrubbed the blood off the deck as the captain in his wheelhouse thought about the prospect of writing yet another death notice letter.

Jack didn't care for violence; in fact, he did everything he could to avoid this war, being amenable as he could to both sides. He met and spoke with General Ulysses S. Grant as well as a passel of Confederate officers including General Nathan Bedford Forrest. Old Jack minded his own business at Bubbling Springs Plantation as long as he could. He stayed out of the war until the actions of a single Union officer dragged him in. And when that happened, there was hell to pay.

After all, John Hinson shared the same customs, values, and traditions of the Scottish clans as his neighbors, notably the law of vengeance. John W. "Old Jack" Hinson settled here sometime before 1850, married Elisabeth (not Elizabeth) James, and established a farm that eventually became a plantation of sorts. Born in North Carolina in July 1807, he traveled west with his family to Tennessee twenty-three years later. There was nothing special about his appearance, being five feet, five inches tall, with one exception. One neighbor remembered in late life, at the age of 105, that Jack had long muscular arms like the newspaper cartoon character Popeye who debuted in 1929.

Years after the Civil War was over, Charles W. Anderson, who served as adjutant general to Confederate general Nathan Forrest, remembered him as having "clear grey eyes, compressed and massive lips," adding that his appearance "clearly indicated that under no circumstances was he a man to be trifled with or aroused." Narrow eyes above high cheekbone, a trait shared to this day with his descendants, known in the family as Hinson eyes, were well suited to the coiled spring of tempered steel that his biographer later discerned from years of study. Then as now, such men are often described in the rural south as "wound up tight."

By 1840, when he was thirty-three, Jack owned ten slaves, reflecting the net worth of a substantial landowner in that place and time. Seven years later, he bought four hundred acres, which he eventually named "Bubbling Springs," a reference to the free flowing water that bubbled out of the ground just behind the house he built there at the headwaters of what became known as Hinson Creek. The structure was large enough to warrant a tavern keeper's license, permitting him to serve meals to overnight guests visiting in the area. His place was on Keel Hollow Road, a major thoroughfare occupying the same space as current US Highway 79.

Before the tragedy, Jack Hinson, uneducated as he was by modern standards, was sophisticated enough to recognize the dangers looming head "between the rivers." Even so, if family stories are to be believed, Jack and his friend John Bell, Southerners though they were, opposed secession and even more strongly against the war to win it. Jack had only hoped that for him and his family, this war would soon be over.

But it wasn't.

Jack Hinson hadn't heard from his son William in some time. Thankfully two of his other sons, George, twenty-two, and John, seventeen, had each decided for reasons of his own to stay at Bubbling Springs at least for the time being, helping do chores around the farm and hunting for meat in the woods that surrounded the place.

Late that fall just before winter began officially on December 21, George and John rose early one morning; breakfasted in the Hinson kitchen; loaded long rifles, shot, powder horns, and game bags; and walked across Hinson Creek looking for game in the stillness before sunrise. Today, the boys would wait for deer and squirrel to arrive in their usual haunts, beneath the birds flying from place to place, scratching out their own breakfasts. Soon the calves bawled and roosters crowed at farms near and far. These familiar sounds that George and John had known their whole lives and no doubt found comforting were soon drowned out by the pounding hooves of the 5th Iowa Cavalry plodding toward their hiding spots in the middle of nowhere, deliberately ending the morning hunt.

The lieutenant in charge led the rest of the Iowans off the path and into the bush, no doubt ordering his men to take the hunting rifles away from George and John. If the usual procedures were followed each of them were tied up, now silently passing from civilians under suspicion to rebels who at that place and time were not entitled to a trial. Less than a mile from Bubbling Springs they were tied to a tree and shot, their protests unheard much less unanswered. The lieutenant then severed their heads or had one of his men do it.

There is no dispute that the bluecoats took the bodies to Dover. Many citizens saw or later said that they saw the bodies of George and John in or near the courthouse square.

An even more dramatic version of events has the brave Iowa Cavalry circling the courthouse square in nearby Dover dragging George and John in the dirt behind them. One variant of this provocative tale has the lieutenant leaving the bodies there but taking the heads to Bubbling Springs.

A local physician, probably Dr. J. W. Smith carried the news and offer of assistance to the Hinson family at Bubbling Springs. Dr. Smith grew up and lived nearby on Lick Creek. And now he brought them bad news and sound advice.

After telling Jack Hinson what happened, Smith related that these brave heroic Iowans would automatically assume that everyone at Bubbling Springs was a traitor; the adults and teenagers among them might well be shot or imprisoned.

One historian characterizes Iowa colonel William W. Lowe as a leader who expected his men to show no mercy whatsoever to local guerillas or their often innocent families, especially when large numbers of weapons were found on their property. Since there was little time to do anything else, before the brave Iowans arrived, Dr. Smith helped Jack Hinson carry all the rifles, shotguns, and ammunition in the Bubbling Springs house and adjoining structures to a nearby maple tree with a hollow trunk. An assortment of scrap iron and old unused farm implements were piled around the tree trunk once it was filled with weapons.

This was the easy part. Jack's wife Elisabeth Hinson no doubt had noticed the commotion and even may have seen Jack and Dr. Smith hiding the weapons. Now she learned that two of her children had been brutally killed.

Within minutes, a blue-coated lieutenant and three enlisted men, one carrying a burlap sack, could be seen through a window trotting toward Bubbling Springs down Hinson Lane. Once on the porch, Smith and Jack Hinson could see the enlisted men placing two bloody objects on the posts of the front-yard gate. As they did so, the lieutenant mounted the porch steps and announced that he was there to arrest and carry away the entire family, since the boys had been caught bushwhacking.

The bluecoats searched and dismantled everything in the house before questioning the slaves, who told them nothing. Disappointed by not finding or hearing what he expected, the blue-coated lieutenant walked past the blood dripping down the gate posts, turned to warn the Hinson family that they would be watched from now on, and rode away.

In the days after the funeral Jack Hinson began to develop a plan, one that had to take into account his age. After all, he was far too old to join the Confederate army as a regular soldier. One thing was certain. Colonel William W. Lowe and many more like him were going to pay for this. Jack pulled his rifles and guns out the tree hollow and began considering what he was going to do and how. His existing Kentucky rifles were all he needed to hunt squirrels, rabbits, and even deer but weren't lethal enough for what he had to do now. In long-distance shooting, his Kentucky rifle would be lethal only when he hit his blue-coated targets squarely in the forehead. What he needed now was a rifle that could deliver a .50-caliber projective, one with a long barrel, heavy enough to pack with one hundred grains or more of black powder. Where would he find such a weapon?

Fortunately for Jack and unfortunately for the bluecoats, some of the best gunsmiths of that time in America lived right here, right in Jack Hinson's home turf, between the Tennessee and Cumberland Rivers. He needed a .50-caliber weapon for long-range accuracy and a very long heavy barrel. This weapon would not be a flintlock. Instead, he needed a rifle with a caplock for quick and easy loading even when the weather was wet.

After making the arrangements for the new rifle to be built, Hinson began making the arrangements for the supplies he would need, making sure that he was not seen buying large quantities of caps and powder. Jack would have to do business with several munitions suppliers. He needed Minié balls with pointed noses for the greatest possible lethal accuracy. The pity was the Union army camped ever so near had Minié balls by the tons, supplies that he could not safely raid. And so he began scouring Stewart County for what he needed.

He started this ammunition quest just down the road from Bubbling Springs in Dover, which he visited from time to time when Union soldiers seemed to be present, allowing Hinson to eventually identify their patterns. He also visited friends near Fort Donelson, now serving as Union headquarters, to learn even more about his adversary. Few of the enlisted men he met from time to time along the road even bothered to nod at this old man of fifty-seven, seeing no threat in him at all.

As time went on he became even more observant, mentally recording their patrol routes, eccentricities when in the saddle, and the leadership qualities (or lack thereof) among Union officers. Slowly, ever slowly digging deeper into their patterns, Jack Hinson memorized their patrol routes, how the enlisted men conducted themselves while in the saddle, and the times when they seemed to be most careless. Soon, he even had profiles on most of the patrol leaders, their practices, strengths, and weaknesses.

Now he began looking at his options for what modern American snipers would call a hide. Since the Yankees now occupied Fort Donelson and Fort Henry, both built by the Southerners, these were not likely spots from which to do any shooting.

Pine Bluff, not to be confused with Pine Bluff, Arkansas, overlooked the Tennessee River downstream from Fort Henry, providing excellent views in both directions, but concealment was poor, since Confederates had cleared much of the timber in the area.

The Dividing Ridge along the Cumberland River side of the land between the rivers provided abundant cover, with places where Hinson could cover his tracks and hide the boats he would be using. Hinson had fewer options south of Dover, where fewer locals lived but the Yankee occupation was stronger.

The area around Leatherwood Creek, on the Tennessee side, was far enough from Union base camps to avoid detection, must less arrest. The woody, hilly terrain there provided many escape routes, not to mention friends and relatives who lived in the area and might provide help if needed. One advantage here was the ability to harass Yankee troops both at Fort Heiman on the Kentucky side and Camp Lowe to the south.

That said, in the end, a high and rugged bluff overlooking the Tennessee River at the mouth of Hurricane Creek in southwest Stewart County became his favorite base of operations for sniping operations. While operating here, Hinson could move from hiding place to hiding place, striking when he could and then moving on to look for fresh opportunities.

Knowing the danger, Hinson hurriedly yet deliberately began planning what was to come, starting with the rifle he needed. Despite his remote area between the two rivers, his specifications were exacting. The rifle would require a full stock made out of a single piece of perfect, tight-grained maple, with which a gunsmith of his choosing would equip a heavy-duty .50-caliber rifled barrel, free from any defects, but that was just the beginning of the process. Once the rifle was constructed the gunsmith would carefully test it, so as to assure himself that the hammer was tight, the trigger soft and smooth, and the breach plug free of any gas leak that might compromise distance or accuracy. After all, Hinson's targets would often be a half mile away.

Fortunately for Hinson, things were not going well at Yankee-occupied Fort Donelson as December 1862 came to an end. Colonel A. C. Harding, commanding officer of the 83rd Illinois Volunteer Infantry had his hands full and then some. When away from the Fort, Harding's men sometimes harassed the local population just to have something to do. The main guardhouse caught fire on January 7, which couldn't be easily blamed on the Confederates in the area or even the local population, being situated as it was smack dab in the middle of the Fort. From time to time, Confederate sharpshooters killed or wounded Harding's men. Prominent among these targets were Virgil and Francis Earp, whose brother Wyatt and friend John Henry "Doc" Holliday became famous nineteen years later at a place in Arizona Territory called Tombstone.

That February, even as Jack made plans to revenge his two sons' deaths, he gave testimony in an inquiry into how exactly how and why Generals John Floyd and Gideon Pillow abandoned Fort Donelson to the Yankee army in early February 1862. His testimony, which nearly mirrored that of General Nathan Bedford Forrest, was particularly important in that unlike the Confederate generals, Hinson had no professional stake in the outcome.

The day after giving testimony in the Fort Donelson hearing, while returning home Jack Hinson passed scores of downcast Confederates, scores of dead horses, and pounds of cannon and other military equipment, the physical remnants of yet another Confederate defeat. Yet instead of accepting the inevitable, Jackson listened to the call of blood for blood, resolved more than ever to avenge his sons' deaths.

Arriving back in Bubbling Springs, he received word that his sniping rifle, almost as tall as Jack himself was ready for action. The weapon featured a full wooden stock, from butt to muzzle made of "tiger maple," a term recognizing the dark stripes throughout the grain of a single piece of maple. The dense barrel, octagonal rather than circular, was 41 inches long, 1.5 inches wide, and bored to the specified .50 caliber with both rear and front sites, customized for long-distance shooting, most importantly including a blade of German steel used to draw a bead on blessedly unsuspecting Yankee targets as far as half a mile away. This rifle was all business. There was no imbedded silver or brass decoration of any kind, only the initials "W.E.G." for William E. Goodman of Lewis County. The lock plate contained a single-word assurance that the weapon was "Warranted" but none of the ornamentation that ordinarily adorned such a high-quality rifle.

The heavy barrel was no coincidence. The density was an absolute requirement to assure long-distance accuracy despite the heavy, unwieldy load of powder required to accurately carry as many as one hundred Minié balls to their Yankee targets. Gunsmith Goodman also made and furnished a bullet mold matched exactly to the dimensions of the rifle bore as was the custom. The whole weapon was designed to force the cone-like Minié ball to expand into the spiraling grooves within the barrel, ideally forcing the projectile out the barrel toward the target with an accuracy similar to that of a spiral pass thrown by a highly skilled quarterback. And in that feature, Jack Hinson's still extant 1863 weapon bears great similarity to competition weapons and sniper rifles made today. These features enabled a typical sharpshooter to accurately hit a target five hundred yards away, ten times the distance that could be accurately covered with the smoothbore musket and spherical ball typically used during the Civil War.

Jack was ready for action but now took specific measures to minimize the risk of detection. Hinson took a loyalty oath that he had no intention of honoring. One might ask how Jack could take such an oath having gone to the trouble and expense of acquiring a sniper's rifle that he soon would shoulder. One distinguished historian has speculated that Jack considered his war against the lieutenant who ordered his sons killed was an act of personal vengeance rather than an act of war against the United States. Perhaps this is so.

Whatever reason Jack used, he began test-firing his new rifle from various distances in various conditions all to one purpose. In the meantime, his son Robert Hinson was arrested in late March 1863 on suspicion of being a Confederate guerilla, suspicions that often led to the suspect simply being shot where he was caught. Robert escaped by crawling out of a window on the second floor of the Stewart County courthouse and climbing down to freedom. This, of course, was a major complication for his father Jack.

There is little doubt that Jack's first sniping mission took place on a quiet spring morning after a quick breakfast, likely consisting of coffee and cold biscuits. His destination was not all that far away. He probably shooed his hunting dogs back to Bubbling Springs, traveled across Hinson Creek and through the woods to the top of a ridge he had picked long before, knowing that the patrol he was waiting to bushwhack would be coming his way in less than an hour. The terrain he crossed and the ridge he descended to his shallow depression overlooking the probable route of the Federal patrol was hardly inviting. In fact, one false or careless step might have meant a fall and an injury, or worse. In all likelihood, he had filled the depression with leaves to provide comfort and cover.

The Yankees would be coming toward him but on a trail so far below his vantage point screened by so much dense foliage that even after the kill shot, they probably wouldn't be able to spot him. And even if they could, there was no path that might allow them to rush up the ridge toward him. Once he had done what he came here to do, he faced a steep climb back up the ridge, but once there, Jack's trip back to the quiet house at Bubbling Springs would likely be trouble free. Or so he might think, perhaps ignoring how this single shot might change his life forever. Whatever his thoughts or reservations at this point, several small but critical tasks had to be taken care of before he heard the horses. His rifle had to be placed across a log, pointed downward toward the trail, with powder flask, Minié ball, and cap box all laid out where these things would be easily accessible when needed, probably knowing that at just that moment, the Yankee patrol was at or near the very place where his boys had been murdered.

While he waited, he would have measured exactly one hundred grains of powder, no more any less, carefully pouring the powder down the muzzle taking care not to spill any. Next, he would wrap a small thin cloth patch around the base of a Minié ball, ram the ball down the barrel of his rifle with a short wooden rod, inexplicably called a starter, take a percussion cap out of a tin box, and, ever so carefully, lower the hammer gently onto the cap. That done, he would make sure that all the gear he had used to get the rifle ready was restored to his shot bag.

And then he waited. No doubt he noticed all the life-stirring birds and animals waking or more often already hunting for the game, plants, and vegetables that might sustain them for yet another day.

Were Jack lucky this morning, he would keep a Yankee officer from seeing another day.

Maybe he heard the horses clambering along, or maybe it was the low yet unmistakable clanking of a sword in its scabbard, keeping time with the rhythm of a horse finding its way along the trail. Whatever the source of the noise, be it human, animal, or both, Jack knew it was time to avenge his boys. Jack no doubt snuggled into the hole he had dug for himself days or even weeks earlier, maybe covering himself with some leaves before carefully, ever so carefully, picking up the Goodman custom rifle and positioning it for the best possible view through the foliage he'd been able to create on earlier trips here. The indistinct murmurs became voices and the voices became the terse words of military language, officers ordering or gently chiding their men forward on the path coming toward Jack and his rifle. The snort of horses struggling beneath their burdens became ever more distinct as Jack no doubt began to think through how and when he would pull the trigger bringing death to at least one Yankee invader.

Tom C. McKenney's intriguing biography *Jack Hinson's One-Man War* that served as the primary source for this chapter reasoned that Hinson now settled in for his first Yankee kill, knowing that he would bring his view into focus by aligning his rifle at the very spot where the first mounted soldier came into view, bringing the silver front sight into alignment with the rear sight making his initial judgments for a target that was a mere half football field away. Now it was only a matter of waiting for that first soldier to appear along the trail.

And when that soldier appeared, Jack Hinson was ready. He quickly cocked the first of the two triggers that had to be set, this one in front, before ever so carefully setting the rear trigger, hoping that he wouldn't inadvertently fire the weapon before the target was within his sight. As Jack Hinson later told the story, he watched the first soldier pass through his sights from right to left, as Hinson quickly assured himself that this was not the lieutenant he was looking to kill. He didn't have long to wait; the second man bore the shoulder patches (called epaulets) that confirmed that this was the man Jack was looking for. Not only that, Jack could see his face as the man glanced at the mounted soldier behind him and then, or so it seemed to Hinson, the lieutenant seemed to peer through the woods, toward the hiding place and into Hinson's eyes, the expression on his face changing the very second Hinson pulled the trigger. Hinson later recalled that the Minié ball struck the lieutenant's throat, pushing him backward over his horse's right flank, his boots still tangled in the stirrups as the horse reared in terror through the spray of blood.

The surviving sergeant ordered his men to dismount and search the slope for the shooter but they found nothing but the smell of gunpowder and a slight aura of smoke, since Jack Hinson was already gone. The dead lieutenant, now bumped along back down the trail toward Fort Donelson, tied to his own horse and accompanied by a small escort, far short of an honor guard, even as Jack carefully and quietly climbed toward the ridge twenty feet or so above him. And from there he walked back down through the forest across Hinson Creek and past the gate posts where the dead lieutenant had displayed his son's heads. According to his principal biographer, Hinson now wondered whether he had really settled accounts with the Yankees or opened the door for more violence.

All too soon he knew the answer. As the spring of 1863 silently turned to summer and his son Robert began operating openly as a Confederate guerilla leader, suspicion increasingly fell on Old Jack himself. Once considered little more than a harmless old man, Hinson now watched an ever increasing number of Yankee patrols combing over his lands and questioning his slaves and his family. Still, life continued on as it had, at least for the time being, surrounded though the Hinson family was by platoon-sized patrols that became company operations and ultimately regimental-sized operations now focusing on the very area where Robert Hanson's guerilla band operated on Wells, White Oak, and Hurricane Creeks. Whatever their size, the Yankee operations began searching for "Hinson's Raiders" either found nothing or pretended that they did.

On Friday, May 8, 1863, a Yankee patrol stumbled into Robert Hinson riding alone along Wells Creek. Robert identified himself by name but claimed he was a Confederate regular, on leave from the 14th Tennessee Infantry Regiment that was then operating in the area. Despite his notoriety and earlier escape, he was not executed on the spot, as some sources suggest happened on a regular basis at this place and time during the war. Instead, he was sent to Nashville for questioning but somehow escaped a second time, this time avoiding the strong possibility of execution. Jack Hinson's biographer suggests that Robert might have benefitted from the fact that the provost marshal clerk in Nashville recorded him as being a member of the 14th Tennessee Cavalry, whose membership included several men named Hinson.

Subsequently, other Union records now began to confuse Robert Hinson with his dead brother George, even as Between the Rivers, Robert Hinson's raiders began accelerating their operations against Union forces, cutting telegraph lines, ambushing the Union forces sent to repair the lines, and attacking selected Union forces in open battles.

May 23 brought new, informal orders from Colonel Lowe at Fort Donelson, who now told the Union adjutant general at Murfreesboro, Tennessee, that he had issued orders "to take no more prisoners." Presumably, this order applied to operations against guerillas rather than regular Confederate forces. Whatever the intended scope of this practice, Colonel Lowe now had a new weapon in his arsenal, a sergeant named George W. Northrup, a once famous frontiersman and scout on the Minnesota–Dakota border.

Northrup was considered so effective that General George Crook assigned him to conduct special operations behind Confederate lines during early 1863. In the meantime, due to the Hinson name confusion, Union forces Between the Rivers now believed that Old Jack Hinson had two living sons active as Confederate guerillas. Consequently, Jack now entertained increasing numbers of Union officers coming to Bubbling Springs. They weren't coming for the water.

Late that June, Robert Hinson was released a 3rd time, confused once again with his dead brother, who the Federals still assumed was still alive, and escaped once again, even as Old Jack plotted more revenge. This time Jack Hinson targeted the enlisted man who pulled his sons' heads out of that burlap sack and mounted them on Jack's gateposts. His was a face that Jack would remember long after the war was over.

An opportunity for revenge against that man, he with the blood-stained hands and sneering smile presented itself while Jack rode toward Bubbling Springs one day. Jack heard and then spotted an outbound Federal patrol; from past experience, he knew about when that patrol would come this way again. But where was that Federal he'd been thinking about? All too soon, the man whose bloodied hands placed George and John's heads on the Hinson gateposts appeared in the middle of the patrol.

Jack knew almost exactly when this patrol would return to Fort Donelson. He had plenty of time to meander along Lick Creek, wander into Dover, and to see and be seen by several of his friends there before returning to Bubbling Springs for his new rifle.

Charlotte Road near the Smith Ford was quiet that evening as sunset approached, but Jack knew he was about to change all that, resting for now beside the long rifle pocketful of ammunition and assorted gear he would need within a very few minutes. Hiding behind a moss-covered log, he began to hear horses plodding along, almost as a predetermined signal that it was time to check the load he had jammed down the rifle barrel, double-check the cap and ease the first hammer down, ever so gently. Soon he was looking over down at the stretch of road that later snipers would call the kill zone, waiting for his target, the barrel of his rifle resting on the log, ready to go. He was concealed from the road; a rising bank would delay the Federals just long enough to allow his escape to the draw nearby where his old mare waited for him.

The Federals now hove into sight, giving Jack an opportunity to adjust his sight and selecting an aiming point, this time, a fork in a small tree that Jack could pretend was his target's head long enough to "bead in" his rifle. This was no casual calculation. Jack had estimated how high his target would be riding on his horse in just a few seconds and adjusted his position accordingly. And now he carefully, ever so carefully, cocked the "set" trigger and pressed his trigger against the trigger guard, just lightly enough to avoid shooting the weapon too soon. Jack assumed that his target would be riding past Jack's hide in the second position after the patrol leader.

The target rode into view just as Jack had expected, with his head turned over his left shoulder talking to the soldier behind him. This Federal was laughing his last laugh ever, looking directly at Jack had he been able to see Jack's concealed position, as Jack aimed at the man's left suspender buckle and barely touched the trigger, knocking that laugh off of the Federal's face in an instant, pushing him backwards off of his horse.

The deed done, Jack disappeared quickly into the draw carrying a cocked pistol just in case, mounted the mare, and rode for Bubbling Springs. He didn't know whether his target was dead but hoped that this would be the end of it, probably knowing in his heart that it wasn't.

His son Robert, often mistakenly identified in Federal records as his dead brother George, became prominent as the leader of a Confederate guerilla band during the summer of 1863, even as Jack's fourth son, William, was furloughed from Confederate service in Virginia and returned home. While William rested at Bubbling Springs, Robert Hinson commanded a Confederate guerilla band that on August 6 seized the telegraph station at Fort Henry, bringing ever more attention to the Confederate sympathies of the Hinson family. Robert was shot to death on September 18 near Fort Donelson while leading his guerilla band on an operation.

Robert was not the only Hinson known to the Confederate command. Jack's reputation might have been the reason Jack Hinson, once friendly with Union general Ulysses Grant, now gave affidavit testimony in a Confederate inquiry as to how and why Confederate fortifications at Fort Donelson and Fort Henry had been so quickly surrendered to Federal forces eighteen months earlier. Now called "Captain" Hinson, despite any official designation as such, Jack Hinson essentially testified in late September or early October 1863 that some eighteen months earlier in February 1862 there had been absolutely no reason to surrender the two Confederate forts to Union forces. Unfortunately for Jack, he was also well known to Federal authorities.

Federal colonel A. A. Smith, who then commanded Fort Donelson nearby, obviously knew about the connection between Confederate guerilla Robert Hinson and his father "Captain" Jack Hinson. He might have also known that William Hinson was on sick leave from the Confederate army staying at Bubbling Springs. That said, following the custom of that time, William was not harassed during his recuperation at Bubbling Springs. He returned to Confederate service in Virginia that January 1864 never to be seen again.

Soon after William left, Colonel Smith decided one afternoon that something had to be done about the Hinson family the very next morning. Somehow word of an impending raid arrived in Dover that evening. Friends in Dover quickly rode to Bubbling Springs and warned Jack and his family. Working quickly, the family was loaded into a snow sled for the twenty-three-mile trip to Sulfur Well where they could stay with relatives. The two youngest children were sick with measles, which then was often fatal.

The next morning, Colonel Smith directed a Union patrol at Fort Donelson to arrest Jack Hinson, burn Hinson's house, and return Hinson to the fort for execution. Family members were to be released unless suspected of treason. The patrol proceeded through deep snow toward Bubbling Springs, where they discovered that the family left hours earlier, leaving the house in the charge of their most trusted servants. Within an hour Bubbling Springs was afire, despite the desperate pleas of the slaves left behind. The lieutenant in charge left the barns intact as a concession.

Jack separated from his westward-traveling family and turned southeast, trying to think through his new life as an outlaw on the run, before turning toward the Danville Crossing area of Middle Tennessee, a heavily wooded area largely inhabited by pro-Confederates who had supported his son Robert's guerilla band. The Crossing was but a village, built to accommodate laborers, engineers, and slaves who arrived there four years earlier to build a railroad bridge across the Tennessee River. It consisted of a steamboat landing, a telegraph terminal, and the oversized Outlaw hotel, built by George or Seth Outlaw. One Confederate officer described Danville Crossing as a fine hotel surrounded by mud. That may have been so, but Jack Hinson now planned to hide out in the area, getting news from time to time at the telegraph terminal. He spent his first night in a cave overlooking the Tennessee River, wondering whether his wife and surviving children found their way to Sulfur Wells.

About twenty feet below a nearby bluff, on a ledge of limestone that his nine-year-old son Charles had engraved the summer before with his own initials, Jack Hinson now planned his hide. The ledge was surrounded by small trees, making it nearly invisible from the Tennessee River two hundred feet below. Of equal importance, as a practical matter this place was unassailable from three sides; there was no easy way for a Federal patrol to get here before Jack could make an escape. Even if they did, the unwary could easily stumble into copperheads and rattlesnakes blocking their path.

In a darkness that came all too soon, he rode for the telegraph terminal at Danville Crossing in search of the news he really didn't want to hear. Loud, boastful Yankees had been bragging about the day's "work" at Bubbling Springs, adding that the entire Hinson family had been branded as enemies. Jack now had a substantial price on his head. While walking along a nearby creek, he decided what had to be done now. His new hiding place would now become a sniping platform.

The next morning he savored all the elements that made his ledge the perfect place to snipe. Most especially, he savored the Towhead Chute and the way in which boats traveling upstream would become almost stationary passing through it, potentially providing him dozens of blue-bellied targets in the weeks to come.

Now he got down to basics, picking specific limbs and branches on which to rest his rifle when shooting before carefully trimming away the absolute minimum amount of vegetation that blocked his view of the river. That done he watered his horse and enjoyed his smoking pipe for a minute or two, until he spotted the first boat. Jack kneeled on his ledge and waited.

That morning in January 1864 marked the second phase of Jack Hinson's career as a Civil War Sniper. According to his own account, he killed the captain of a US Navy gunboat laden with military cargo.

Hinson could see that the crew was not concerned about Confederate marksman along the river banks. In fact, many of them looked at the cliffs along the Tennessee River as if they were modern-day tourists on a cruise boat.

Hinson shot the navy captain in his left side, slamming the man to his knees with blood pouring from his left chest and the exit wound on his right side. He was dead within minutes, even as a medical orderly went through the motions of bandaging him.

A few days later, Hinson spotted a southbound troop transport steaming upstream with a deck full of lounging army officers. The army officer Hinson picked to die that day was smoking a pipe and talking, as a group of other army officers around him appeared to listen. Just as the army captain pointed to something on the hillside, possibly even Jack himself, the bullet struck him mid-chest, knocking him backward and down onto a deck that soon would be stained with his blood. The bullet spent itself in the leg of a lieutenant who was standing behind him.

A few days later another navy boat lumbered into Towhead Chute, announced in advance by black chimney smoke rising silently above the crest of nearby hills with supplies bound for Johnsonville, Tennessee. While the boat struggled upstream in the Towhead Chute, Old Jack scanned the quarterdeck, settling at last on the boat captain, then pointing at something just ahead which the Union officer wanted his crew to see. Hinson's bullet drove the captain to his knees even as his face hit the wheelhouse wall, where he slumped as if in deep prayer, as perhaps he was. Within seconds he was dead. Jack's work for the day was done.

Eventually, Hinson marked the occasion by engraving a small circle in the barrel of his sniping weapon. He engraved another thirty-one circles before the war came to an end. After a few days' rest, he moved his sniping operation to a location closer to Sulfur Wells so that he could spend more time with his family between killings. Now operating on the west side of the Tennessee River, he learned that his two youngest children had died from measles shortly after leaving Bubbling Springs. Within days, he happened upon two Union soldiers who told him they were looking for Jack Hinson. Jack was helpful or seemed to be, telling the Union men that he himself had seen Jack Hinson less than an hour ago on a logging road near Standing Rock Creek. Jack gave them the longest most time-consuming route there.

The ambush site was quiet enough when Jack arrived, long before the Union soldiers looking to kill or capture him for the reward money. Once there, he looked about for a sniping hide, found a downed tree with a view, and waited. Jack listened for the snorting and blowing that told him that his targets had slowed their horses from a gallop to a trot and then a walk. The challenge, Jack knew, would be to kill them both. The first shot would be easy, but could he reload quickly enough to take out the second target before he galloped away or, worse yet, up the slope to Jack's hide? Jack could reload in an amazing six seconds, but in combat, six seconds can be a lifetime or life's end.

Jack didn't have much time to consider all this before he cocked the hammer, squeezed the set trigger, and aimed exactly where he expected to see the upper chest of the first soldier approaching him.

Then he set his "sight picture" so that the rear sight, the front sight, and the target were all in perfect alignment. Once this was done, he would have taken several breaths, waited for the first horse to appear, raised his aim upward to chest height on the first target, taken a final breath, let half of that breath out, and touched (not squeeze) the trigger. Later, Jack remembered his bullet striking the first target between his right shoulder and his breastbone, throwing him off the horse, the target's right lung and the large blood vessels just above his heart torn asunder.

Now the pressure was really on as Jack quickly pushed the rifle under his armpit, tore the powder load open with his teeth, poured the powder down the muzzle without spilling any, pushing a Minié ball down the muzzle behind the powder, ramming the entire load down the barrel cocking the trigger, and placing the rifle on a log where he could fire it again, just before the second soldier aimed his cumbersome dragoon pistol at Jack to fire, a second too late. Jack's bullet struck the soldier in the center of his upper chest, or so Jack remembered, knocking the man off the side of his horse. The Union soldier was still tangled in the right stirrup as his horse ran back the way he came a few yards and simply stopped.

All Jack could hear now was the pawing and stomping of both horses, trained as they had been to remain stationary as crows circled and cried from high above. Jack found the first man lying directly beneath his horse already dead. The second soldier hanged dead from his horse, his right foot tangled in the stirrup.

During the rest of the war, Hinson killed navy and army officers on Federal boats traveling along the Tennessee and Cumberland Rivers. According to his own account, on one occasion he killed so many officers on the deck of an armed transport ship that the surviving captain sent up the white flag of surrender, perhaps thinking that the vessel was confronted with an entire company of snipers.

In October 1864, Hinson served as a scout for Confederate general Nathan Bedford Forrest. His son William never returned from Confederate service in Virginia, but Jack and the rest of his family lived on. "Old Jack" Hinson died in late July 1874 at age sixty-seven, in the month of his birth.

CHAPTER FIVE

Muskrats in Blue

WE HAVE SEEN THAT THE US ARMY VALUED THE SKILLS OF sharpshooters almost from the beginning of its history. The inception of the Civil War brought new emphasis on these skills.

At least three Union generals were arguably killed by Confederate sharpshooters. Generals John F. Reynolds, Stephen W. Weed, and Strong Vincent were killed in or near Gettysburg in early July 1863. Forty years later, fifty-six-year-old Benjamin Thorpe of Satterwhite, North Carolina, told a reporter from the *Los Angeles Herald* that a Confederate officer had directed him to climb to the top of a cherry tree on the Gettysburg battlefield and shoot General Reynolds on July 1, 1863. Reynolds was about nine hundred yards away, when it happened, according to Thorpe. In Thorpe's 1903 telling of the story, he was among some one hundred sharpshooters hidden among the trees with orders to take out any Union officers from their perches just below Seminary Ridge. Reynolds was galloping along Emmitsburg Road when Ben Thorpe's Confederate lieutenant spotted him. "Ben, do you see the tall, straight man in the center of that group?" the officer asked. "He is evidently an officer of some high rank and is directing operations which threaten our line. Sight your gun at 700 yards and see if you can reach him." And so he did. Thorpe waited patiently for the officer to see what happened.

"That's a little short Ben," said the officer, giving him new distance directions. "Hold steady, for we must have him." Recalling what happened forty years earlier, Thorpe told the Los Angeles newspaper in 1903 that he sighted his long-barreled rifle at the range given, steadied it on a limb, aimed, and fired. This time, Thorpe's rifle ball hit Reynolds in the side of the head. "I knew before the report died away, before I saw General Reynolds fall that the shot had been a good one and would reach its mark." Neither ebullient nor boastful, Thorne told the *Herald* reporter that he had regretted that killing from the day it happened.

That may be so, but both Union and Confederate generals recognized the military value of sharpshooters from the very beginning of the conflict. And so it is no surprise that soon after the war began Union officers asked New York engineer and championship marksman Hiram Berdan to organize a regiment of marksman. Berdan's Sharpshooters became the best known and "the most celebrated marksmen in the Union ranks."

Even so, one little-known regiment might have equaled or exceeded Berdan's men, as skilled as they were. According to its regimental history, the 9th New Jersey Volunteer Infantry once outperformed Berdan's Sharpshooters in a team marksmanship competition. The 9th, nicknamed the Muskrats for reasons we will explore later, has been described as arguably the most distinguished of the forty regiments of infantry New Jersey contributed to the Union army. Raised as a sharpshooting regiment and clothed in green-trimmed blue uniforms, even the most astute Civil War contemporary observer knew little or nothing about them.

According to the historian Edward G. Longacre, whose 2017 work *The Sharpshooters: A History of the 9th New Jersey Volunteer Infantry in the Civil War* is largely relied upon in this chapter, these outdoorsmen and target shooters were largely unknown to the public in their own day and have remained almost anonymous due to serving mostly in North Carolina, a campaign largely overlooked until recent years by most Civil War historians.

The regiment may have earned the nickname "Jersey Muskrats" during an expedition led by General Ambrose E. Burnside in 1862, but the source and meaning of this nickname remains controversial to this day.

Throughout the war, the New Jersey Muskrats did heavy, serious damage to every Confederate unit that opposed them, in and around Charleston, South Carolina, during the spring of 1863 and Southern ("Southside") Virginia in mid-1864. On April 14, 1861, the day Fort Sumter surrendered to Confederate forces, pranksters in Belvidere (not Belvedere), New Jersey, raised the South Carolina flag prompting a local newspaper headline "SECESSION IN BELVIDERE."

The idea was not as astonishing as it might seem. Hundreds of Southerners vacationed annually in New Jersey, while the College of New Jersey, eventually renamed Princeton, educated much of the southern aristocracy of that time. Several hundred New Jersey natives served in the Confederate army; four were generals. And, of course, bigotry and racism were not constrained by the Mason–Dixon Line.

The New Jersey Muskrats shared the view of many Union soldiers but were more articulate than most in describing underfed, ill-equipped Confederate soldiers as scarecrows and ragamuffins. There was also room in the generally abolitionist views of 9th Regiment soldiers for racist comments about black freeman and slaves. While eager for the enemy intelligence such blacks might provide, some in the regiment went out of their way to describe the former slaves they encountered as "sassy" and even "pampered." Worse still, during the Carolina campaigns, 9th Regiment members denounced black soldiers serving under conditions that might best be described as difficult at best as poorly disciplined, disgraceful, and unfit to wear the Union uniform. At least one letter from a 9th veteran described blacks he encountered with frequent use of the "n" word.

Despite this, when Lincoln's mid-April 1861 call for volunteers came, the initial New Jersey quota was quickly and easily exceeded. The first call specifying sharpshooters came from Colonel Hiram Berdan, a mechanical engineer who had already gained a reputation as "the finest rifleman in prewar America." His organization eventually became a regiment known as the "First US Sharpshooters." After a second such regiment called Berdan's Sharpshooters but not commanded by him, Charles Scranton and other New Jersey leaders persuaded the US War Department for authorization to organize and recruit for the 9th New Jersey. A broadsheet (modern term "flyer") dated September 17 solicited one hundred men to serve in a company of 9th Regiment "Sharp Shooters." A company consisting of men between eighteen and thirty-six years of age, "all good marksmen," was recruited in the broadsheet. Two weeks later, Elias J. Drake was authorized to raise a second such company.

The recruits largely volunteered from the rural and coastal areas of New Jersey, where men were "accustomed to the use of firearms from boyhood." Many were experienced woodsmen and watermen. Two other companies, these from urban Newark, were largely drawn from German-born veterans of European wars.

Nearly forty years later, a regimental historian nostalgically remembered the regiment as largely consisting of "bright-faced men in the hey-day of their youth" who had "left their happy homes on the mountains as well as from hamlets embosomed in picturesque valleys, where freemen grow stalwart and their souls on fire with love of country. They came from the cabins which dot the sandy beach from Monmouth to Cape May . . . from cottages by the riverside and among the artificial streams [canals] . . . from the lines of the railways . . . from college, office, workshop, mill and factory determined to lend their best efforts in resisting the reckless men who were striving to subvert their nation's liberties."

The first group, largely German immigrants and second-generation German-Americans reached Camp Olden, named for the New Jersey governor and located on the outskirts of Trenton, on Friday, September 13.

Within a few weeks, the men of the 9th New Jersey were trained in the bare fundamentals of military discipline and tactics. Now, they waited impatiently for orders and arms while feasting on abundant high-quality food in good variety. Although many brought their own weapons with them, the regiment as a whole was unarmed. Finally, a shipment of bargain basement .69-caliber smoothbore Belgian muskets with a maximum range of only two hundred yards recently purchased in Europe arrived at Camp Ogden. Finally, on November 26, the regiment received some one thousand Model 1861 Springfield rifles, capable of hitting targets six hundred yards away with a .58-caliber Minié ball. Eight days later, the 9th New Jersey was dispersed among three separate trains chugging toward Washington, DC, via Camden, Philadelphia, and Baltimore. Soon, the 9th New Jersey was camped next to Berdan's Sharpshooters on Meridian Hill, which then and now provides a dramatic view of Washington from the Northwest Quadrant. Before Christmas, a selected team of New Jersey sharpshooters bested a team from Berdan's Regiment in a marksmanship contest, or so the story goes.

Ten days after Christmas, the 9th New Jersey was on a January 4 train bound for an expedition into North Carolina led by General Ambrose E. Burnside. Late on the afternoon of January 5, some of them hurried aboard a transport named the *Anne E. Thompson* and the brigantine *Dragoon*, to sail with an eighty-ship flotilla for North Carolina.

Their objective was Roanoke Island, the destination of a "lost colony" founded in 1585 by Sir Walter Raleigh. The next year, Roanoke Island colonists returning with Sir Francis Drake introduced tobacco, corn, and potatoes to England. The remaining colonists disappeared by 1587, most likely as a consequence of conflicts with the Native Americans who initially helped them.

Now, in mid-January 1862, the Union objective was to seize Roanoke Island, providing General Ambrose E. Burnside a thoroughfare of sorts providing easy access to a Confederate communications hub at Norfolk and enemy railroad links to Virginia, if only the weather would clear.

During a brief interlude on the morning of the fifteenth the wind was light enough for Colonel Allen, then commanding the 9th to row ashore with several others, report to General Burnside, and perhaps get the *Thompson* and the *Dragoon* towed into anchorage so that the men could go ashore. Whether or not permission was granted, as Allen and the others were rowed back to the Thompson they encountered angry breakers the last of which swept everyone into the water.

Colonel Allen weighed down by a moat of India rubber and surgeon Frederick S. Weller drowned along with a seaman, despite heroic efforts to save them all.

Two days after this tragedy, the *Thompson* and the *Dragoon* still rode high waves aggravated by high winds many miles from the safe harbor Allen and Weller had died trying to obtain. The *Pawtuxet* sent to rescue the *Dragoon* almost did so, but the Dragoon struck bottom just outside the inlet and would have foundered had General Burnside not personally brought his own vessel out to tow the *Dragoon* to safety. Three days later, despite some difficulties, the *Thompson* and the rest of the 9th New Jersey joined her at Hatteras Inlet. And there they remained until came February.

Confederate brigadier General Henry A. Wise recounted in his memoir that Roanoke Island was "the key to all the rear defenses of Norfolk," which "unlocked two sounds . . . eight rivers . . . four canals" and two railroads.

Looking back with perfect hindsight, Wise thought the strategic importance of the island would have justified a defense consisting of at least 20,000 men, rather than the 1,400 effectives commanded by Colonel Henry M. Shaw of the 8th North Carolina Infantry. Yet, North Carolina ("the Old North State") never achieved first-tier status in Confederate military thinking. Only thirteen thousand marginally trained and equipped troops had to cover the entire four-hundred-mile North Carolina coastline, supported by a Southern-engineered naval squadron commanded by William F. Lynch consisting of five tugboats and two side-wheel steamers converted into warships carrying an aggregated nine guns. There were at least five water batteries of cannon, three of which came into play during the coming battle.

The naval battle for the island began at noon, followed by an infantry attack in the late afternoon, at Ashby's Harbor. Although a well-intentioned runaway slave recommended this landing site, it was covered by Confederate sharpshooters well hidden in woods nearby. Burnside rapidly adjusted his battle plan to use a virtually unguarded adjacent stretch of beach for his offensive.

Union brigadier general John Gray Foster landed his four-thousand-member command there at about 4:00 p.m. The 9th New Jersey followed them by rowboat just after the sun set at 5:39 p.m. in the midst of a heavy blowing rain. Strangely enough, as soon as they landed, the men sensed that they were not on firm ground at all. Instead, they were forced to find their way to land amidst bogs, patches of knee-deep mud, sea grass, and even wet sand, at last finding a firm open space where they could camp in a cold, drizzling rain, without blankets or knapsacks, much less tents. Burnside's entire command was onshore by midnight to savor the conquest of Roanoke with hardly a Confederate shot being fired.

February 8, a Saturday, dawned chilly and fog-covered, but Burnside's scouts could travel and see well enough to report that the area that Burnside's forces occupied was relatively Confederate-free. That said, Shaw's regiment as well as the 31th North Carolina and most of the Seventeenth and two of Wise's regiments had consolidated. On the positive side, the Confederate artillery batteries were too far away to be effective.

Burnside now concentrated on his next objective: a makeshift earthwork that the Confederates had spread across the three-mile-wide "waist" of the island. Reconnaissance indicated that the very center of the earthworks featured a battery of three antiquated yet useable smoothbore guns of Mexican vintage for which the Rebels had ammunition, as well as an additional piece the Confederates could not use.

Shaw knew that this was the likely Federal objective. His hope, at least in the short term rested on three infantry units featuring six companies from North Carolina and Virginia regiments stationed behind breastworks facing the Yankees and on the edge of a swamp that at least in theory protected Shaw's left flank. A small, mobile reserve unit completed this hodge-podge. Many of Shaw's men were armed with double-barreled shotguns and antique flintlock muskets.

Throughout the previous night, Burnside and other Union officers developed the plan of attack to conquer Shaw's earthwork.

Foster's brigade led the attack as planned at 7:30 a.m. but most of them squeezed onto a muddy causeway across the island made worse by recent rains. They soon became so bogged down that Burnside called for Reno's Brigade, the 3rd element of which was the 9th New Jersey, many of whom complained loudly at being kept out of the battle, at least until some of the earliest casualties were carried toward them on stretchers.

Sometime after 8:00 a.m. General Reno gave them the chance many in the 9th had been looking for, ordering them to enter the swamp on the left flank. The column led directly by Colonel Charles A. Heckman, a forty-year-old, dark-headed Pennsylvanian with an extraordinarily long mustache, plunged quickly and noisily into swamp waters coming to their waists or higher. Worse still, as they walked through this mud, tree boughs and branches fell from above onto their heads.

More than a few of the 9th New Jersey men noticed how calmly Heckman led his men into battle, exposing himself to fire. One man later recalled that Heckman "stood up and faced a shower of balls thicker than any hail storm," leading the way to firmer ground at a tree line only one hundred yards away from the enemy lines. They faced a dilemma many of them would never forget. "We could hardly penetrate the undergrowth," one 9th New Jersey veteran remembered years later, saying that it was "such as no man need ever wish to experience again."

Here again, Heckman had planned ahead, placing many of the better 9th New Jersey sharpshooters in front to inflict as much early damage as possible on the Rebels. Many of the 9th New Jersey men were ready for this action. "I felt as cool as and no more excited than if I had been shooting birds in the woods," one man recalled.

The Confederates were hardly expecting this. Those closest to the 9th New Jersey seemed entirely unprepared for what had happened. Even when Colonel Shaw had one of his guns repositioned to reduce the Confederate carnage, New Jersey lieutenant colonel Heckman had his best sharpshooters take out the gunners.

Lieutenant William B. Selden, a member of Shaw's staff, was one Rebel prepared for battle. Heckman watched Selden reload and fire a cannon just as several New Jersey sharpshooters fatally shot him. The cannon that Selden had fired killed four Union men and permanently disabled two others.

About two hours later, a 9th Lieutenant climbed a pine tree and observed Rebels begin abandoning their earthworks, giving the Union regiments just enough time to charge at the best possible moment, causing panic in Rebel ranks during the retreat. Soon, Shaw and his Confederates surrendered the island. The 9th took possession of an abandoned Rebel barrack for the evening, complete with cooked meals on the stove. Despite their fatigue, the 9th New Jersey and the rest of the Union forces joined in an evening soiree featuring General Reno or another general officer who claimed that the Rebels were broken and the war (yes, the war) would soon be over.

According to some accounts, this was the very time when the Union army began calling the 9th New Jersey "Jersey Muskrats." Or did they? There is little dispute that the men of the 9th earned the nickname by swimming and fighting at the same time. The question is, when, where and by whom was this unwieldy nickname conferred? Six weeks after this February 9 battle a corporal Stillwell wrote that General Ambrose Burnside himself named the 9th New Jersey "Muskrats" when he watched the regiment swim through mud up to their necks. J. Madison Drake, then a sergeant, later claimed in his regimental history that captured Confederates, highly impressed by the aquatic abilities of the 9th were the first to call them "muskrats" but no independent corroboration has ever surfaced. Yet another tale ascribed the first use of the term to a Confederate colonel who had seen the 9th in action at Roanoke Island. During a later battle, he supposedly said that "the quicker we get out of here, the better, for them damned muskrats will go through that swamp in spite of hell." During the March 14 Battle of Bern, the 9th attacked Confederate positions by wading through waist-deep swamps, sometimes swimming toward the enemy objective as necessary. Corporal Symmes Stilwell, yet another source of information about the regiment, claimed years later that the Confederates called them the "Bloody Ninth." The most recent 9th New Jersey regimental history states that the 9th earned the moniker during the March 14 Battle of Bern, wading through waist-deep swamps, sometimes swimming toward the Confederate position.

Reader's choice.

By early March the Muskrats received orders for a new, undisclosed mission, now that the North Carolina coast had been secured by Union forces. Rumors flying from camp to camp strongly suggested that the next target would be New Bern, then the second-largest city in the state with a population of some 5,400 at the confluence of the Neuse and Trent Rivers. New Bern was a perfect haven for privateers bringing in the vital supplies and armaments necessary to keep the Rebellion alive, despite the efforts of the North Atlantic Blockading Squadron.

Dawn March 3 brought news that the 9th New Jersey and the rest of the Union force would be boarding Burnside's own "flagship," the steamer *Peabody* as well as the old reliable *Dragoon* and two new ships, the *H.F. Brown* and the *Albany*. Due to inclement weather, they remained on the North Carolina coast until the morning of March 12, when the transport flotilla, now accompanied by several gunboats tacked for the mouth of the River Neuse, anchoring for the night at 8:00 p.m. while the warships sailed on to New Bern intent upon taking out the local defenses there.

The next morning they began the fourteen-mile hike through low marshy ground toward their objective: the Rebel left front and center. Reno's troops would attack the right flank. Their 9:00 p.m. campout was near enough to Confederate pickets that the two sides exchanged pleasantries and insults throughout the night.

The Union objective was works located some six miles south of New Bern defended by yet another undersized Confederate force of some 4,500, anchored on the right by the 26th North Carolina Infantry, the best led, best trained of the lot. Former newspaper editor and congressman Lawrence O'Bryan Branch, now a brigadier general, commanded the entire Confederate force. All the forces directly under Burnside's command, including the 9th New Jersey, began their initial advance against the Confederate right on the evening of the thirteenth and resumed at daybreak the next morning, slogging through sand and mud before breakfast.

A few hundred yards into the march, the advance elements of the 9th New Jersey could see the Rebel works and the shooting commenced. Soon, the Muskrats were doing what they had been recruited for: sharpshooting. In the far distance, they could see Confederate heads peeking out above the enemy works, and a few firing from trees, while they themselves were still exposed to small arms fire. The Muskrats picked off more than a few Rebel tree snipers, while swinging into line just in time to keep Confederates on the left from flanking the entire Union force. Within a few minutes, the Muskrats had also silenced a Confederate artillery battery about one hundred yards away in a ravine and picked off an officer in charge of one of the guns. One Muskrat claimed that he had known the dead Confederate captain before the war, a story, however dubious, that was published nationally. Before the day was done and the battle won, the 9th had captured six enemy artillery pieces and even a dead officer's horse.

On June 11, the Reverend Thomas Mann, a Baptist clergyman in New Bern with strong Unionist tendencies, was kidnapped, perhaps as revenge for ministering to the men of the 9th. Rumor had it that Mann was being held in Swansborough, some forty-two miles to the south of New Bern, on the other side of the massive Croatan forest. A consolidated force that included several Muskrats marched to his rescue, found the Rebel barracks abandoned, and burned it. So far as is known, the Union army never located the good reverend.

The Muskrats spent the next month in bored frustration, unable as they had been to capture, much less kill, any Confederate raiders. Finally, an opportunity to do just that came in late July when General Foster directed four separate scouting missions to find and destroy Confederate forces. The first three, conducted by other Unionists, were unsuccessful. Finally, a mixed force including the Muskrats and elements of the 3rd New York Cavalry and the New York Rocket (artillery) Battalion led by Colonel Heckman marched out before dawn on July

26 for Young's Cross Roads, some twenty-five miles away. Reaching their destination by noon the next day, the combined Heckman forces were ambushed almost immediately by Rebels who burned a bridge to keep from being captured, all to no avail. The 9th captured some twenty prisoners. Before returning to New Bern, some of the Muskrats burned the home of a Confederate officer, without any objection from Heckman.

In the weeks that followed, seemingly peaceful civilians operating as bushwhackers at night now harassed the Muskrats. Even as such attacks increased, the overall health of the regiment declined, due to typhoid, fevers, and weather-related maladies. Still and all, the Muskrats saw plenty of sharpshooting from time to time.

A mixed force evening mission on August 14 to scout a Rebel stronghold back in Swansborough, some thirty miles southwest of Newport Barracks (in present-day Newport), typifies the challenges now ever frequently confronting the Muskrats. The mission conducted by one hundred men from the 9th New Jersey with two companies of New York Cavalry was described by one newspaper reporter as the quickest march of its kind ever conducted.

A detailed reconnaissance required crossing the White Oak River by boat, but two gunboats towing barges with cannons never appeared the next morning. Having no other options, Colonel Heckman had the Muskrats search the nearby riverbanks for anything that could float. All that could be found was an old two-masted sailboat and a single canoe, with combined seating for only sixteen troops. Company M captain Joseph M. McChesney and fifteen of his Muskrats piled into the vessels. They nearly reached the lower wharf at Swansborough without interference, but at the last minute they were spotted. The small force they expected to confront instead consisted of several hundred well-armed Confederates. The Muskrats dispersed some of them with well-placed volleys, but the small Muskrat force now faced three boatloads of angry Rebels rowing furiously into the river to cut them off, but to no avail. On the way back to Newport Barracks, they burned several houses belonging to "known secessionists" and confiscated a large number of weapons.

The 9th New Jersey participated in an expedition to Tarboro, North Carolina, personally led by General Foster to retaliate for recent Confederate actions against coastal garrisons at Washington (regionally called Little Washington) and Plymouth, Virginia. The action began for the Muskrats on the evening of October 29, 1862. Four days later, Rebel marksman brought the Federal expedition to an abrupt halt just short of a swamp two miles from Rowell's Mill. After the Rebels repulsed the 24th Massachusetts skirmishers, General Foster began calling for the "one regiment here that can cross that swamp."

"Bring up the Muskrats!" Foster shouted, and within a few minutes, Colonel Heckman led the 9th New Jersey to the front of the column. Despite heavy opposing fire, the Muskrats soon shoved the Rebels across the creek. Next, the 9th New Jersey crossed a burning bridge and chased the Confederates on the other side until darkness fell.

Thirteen days before Christmas, General Foster assigned the Muskrats to seize a major railroad bridge over the Neuse River at Goldsboro, North Carolina, a remote yet vital Confederate communications center at the junction of two major railroads that carried rations, arms, and ammunition to Lee's army in Virginia. Foster intended to destroy the railroad bridge and as much railroad track at the junction as conditions permitted. On most days, the 9th New Jersey would be leading an expedition that included a battalion of the 3rd New York Cavalry and a battery of Rhode Island Light Artillery.

On the morning of the thirteenth, the expedition confronted and faced down a Confederate force at Southwest Creek. Some six weeks earlier, Rebels had destroyed most of the bridges in the area, but now the Muskrats led the expedition across the creek, using felled trees as floats and doing some swimming, prompting the Rebel commander to retreat. The next morning, a few miles short of a railroad bridge over the Neuse River, Rebel skirmishers took a defensive position, which the Muskrats countered with a bayonet charge, driving the Rebels across the all-important bridge. Then the rebels set the bridge on fire.

This was only a temporary problem for the Muskrats, who used artillery sponge buckets filled with water to douse the fire and, in most but not all accounts, took the lead crossing the still smoldering bridge, in a close race with the 10th Connecticut. Shortly thereafter, the Union soldiers captured several hundred Rebel prisoners, four cannon, and the battle flag of a South Carolina regiment. One Jersey man later recalled that the Rebels spent five days after the battle burying their dead.

Mid-afternoon found the 9th entering Kinston (not Kingston), twenty-eight miles southeast of Goldsboro, home to 1,300 souls, pillaged by fellow Union soldiers moments earlier. One observer noted that every bar of soap and razor in the barber shop was taken.

The Muskrats spent December 16 and 17 engaged with Confederate forces desperate to save the Rebel communication center at Goldsboro, first engaging them at nearby White Hall, also known as Whitehall or White Hall Ferry. Here the 9th Virginia found yet another bridge crossing the Neuse, fortified this time by heavy breastworks and extensive rifle pits on both sides of the river. The rebels occupied a thirty-foot bluff from which Confederate sharpshooters in the trees picked off Union officers, some swinging from ropes in the large pines.

The Muskrats led the expedition once again on the seventeenth, moving behind skirmishers toward the covered 220-yard-long railroad bridge over the Neuse on the outskirts of Goldsboro, which the Union commanders had ordered destroyed, in the face of Confederate orders to hold it at all costs. Five Muskrat volunteers assembled artillery fuses and began moving toward the bridge despite furious continuous Rebel fire. Only when they reached their objective did the Union men discover that they had no way to ignite the fuses they dragged all this way. Private Elias Winans volunteered for a potentially fatal run into the nearby woods for twigs and leaves that might or might not set the fuses on fire. Winans finished that task and then piled everything flammable he had on the wooden abutment, the substructure keeping the bridge intact. According to eyewitnesses, once Winans ignited the leaves and artillery fuses, the bridge was ablaze in a matter of minutes, even as other regiments that accompanied the 9th New Jersey were destroying both railroad tracks at this important junction.

Despite the Muskrat exuberance, somber news reached them that day from the Army of Potomac. A disastrous defeat at Fredericksburg,

Virginia, some 224 miles to the north, suggested to General Foster that the expedition should return to New Bern as soon as possible. They arrived on the afternoon of the twentieth, after covering some thirty-two miles and achieving their mission in only twelve hours. The cost had been high. Over one hundred casualties had been sustained in four separate battles or skirmishes over the past ten days.

The Muskrats spent the beginning days of 1863 recuperating, drilling, practicing their sharpshooting, and training new recruits for what was to come. In the meantime, Colonel Heckman received the promotion to brigadier general he so richly deserved; the New Jersey legislature sent a new flag recognizing their accomplishments at Roanoke and Newbern. Perhaps as a consequence of inaction, their marksmanship in mid-March 1864 was in serious decline.

The service term for the 9th New Jersey would end in September 1864, but efforts began the preceding November to keep the regiment intact. January found over five hundred regiment men reenlisted and renamed the 9th New Jersey as Volunteer Veteran Infantry, now serving in Virginia.

A minor Virginia skirmish on March 1 near the Dismal Swamp Canal, not far from Deep Creek, just south of Portsmouth, interrupted a peaceful early 1864 interlude. The action started when twenty-five Muskrat skirmishers were sent forward to intercept a small number of dismounted Rebel horsemen lying in wait along the Bear Quarter Road only to find at least 150 and perhaps as many as 500 Confederates waiting for them. Rebels killed two of the three-man advance guard and then stripped and mutilated one of the bodies. Even so the Muskrats and elements of the 8th Connecticut, some 950 men in all chased the Confederates across the North Carolina line.

Two months later on May 12, the Muskrats led a large portion of General Butler's army from Bermuda Hundred to attack some five thousand Confederates at Drewry's Bluff, seven miles away on a plank-road turnpike. The Muskrats scouted out Rebel skirmishers, not knowing that one of their most important sniping assignments of the war lay just two days ahead of them.

When a contingent from the 9th led the advance toward small rivulet called Kingsland Creek early on the morning of Saturday, May 14, they drew fire, reported what they saw, and were soon joined by General Hickman himself. The Union forces, Hickman discovered, were confronted by a line of breastworks. And between the breastworks and the Muskrats was a long line of obstacles (called abatis) made of tree branches laid in a row, with the sharpened tops directed toward the Federals. The abatis stretched as far as the eye could see. Muskrat Companies D and G climbed over the abatis and used portions of the fortification as sniper hides from which they shot at the Rebels, with great effect. Later, it was said that the Muskrats spent a leisurely afternoon picking off Rebels who dared lift their heads above the breastworks.

The next day passed all too quietly as Confederates just out of sight were moving men, material, and artillery into place across the entire battle line. The Muskrats were moved for reasons unknown at dusk to the far right of the Union line near the James River and ordered to immediately begin digging in despite the fact that they lacked the necessary tools to do so effectively. Consequently, the fortifications consisted solely of tree trunks, limbs, and stumps haphazardly and quickly put into place. On the far right, some four hundred yards in front of the Muskrats, stood the home of one R. A. Willis, located high enough to provide a commanding view of the battlefield. Brigadier General Heckman who had commanded the 9th realized that even this was not enough.

He urged General William Farrar ("Baldy") Smith to reinforce what he argued to be "the most important point in the whole line, as it covered the shortest route to our [the Union's] base of supplies, and on its retention depended the safety of the Union army."

The Confederate offensive against the Muskrat position started almost casually, with intermittent seemingly half-hearted attacks on the Willis house by dismounted cavalry, graduating to full-throated Rebel yells, concluding at 5:00 a.m. on the fog-shrouded dawn with infantry rushing forward. Henry Keenan, one of the better, more aggressive sharpshooters among the Muskrats, recalled that soon "volleys came from the house. It was plain we could do nothing. I don't know who gave the order to retreat, but by a common impulse, as the mass of rebels became clearly defined by the flashes of their own guns; we turned and ran toward the main line, a 3rd of a mile behind us." One Muskrat later recalled the fog-shrouded chaos that dawn: "We could not tell our men from the rebels until we got close to them." "Only when the enemy was a few feet away," another Muskrat remembered, could they make out "their grey and motley dress and emaciated features . . . and we could deliver our fire with telling effect."

The Muskrats could not know that the Confederate vanguard was led by Brigadier General Archibald Gracie III of Elizabeth, New Jersey. Eventually, Gracie's four infantry regiments broke the 9th New Jersey lines, setting the stage for what seemed to be hour upon hour of sharpshooting, from distances sometimes as close as twenty feet. At times, Private Henry Keenan recalled, he could hear Rebel officer orders more clearly than Muskrat voices. Keenan's rifle became so foul from constant use that he used two others pried from the hands of dead and injured comrades nearby, until Keenan himself was shot in the head. Before that Keenan watched the Muskrat's own Colonel Zabriskie, himself shot in the throat, relinquish command to Colonel James Stewart, the last field-grade officer left on that segment of the Union line. Soon, Stewart was shot in the thigh and passed command to (Captain) Sam Hufty. Despite the severity of his head wound, Keenan survived and returned to fight again, five months later.

Just as General Heckman could have predicted, across their entire segment of the line, Muskrats were now compelled by the sheer force of arms to give way, as New York–born General Gracie pushed his Alabamans around them. Unanchored, at least for the moment, the 9th New Jersey retreated as ordered by General Heckman, although some individual Muskrats, including Sergeant Meyers and Lieutenant Frederick Coyte, refused the order, at least momentarily, and tried, unsuccessfully, to rally. During the chaos, most of the 9th New Jersey men in Companies D and G were taken prisoner.

The Union army leadership began thinking seriously about a full retreat, at least until the morning fog burned away, revealing that Beauregard's once invincible offensive had ground to a halt, just as virtually the entire Federal army returned to the original line of defense to fight another day. Some 150 of the Muskrats were dead and wounded. Colonel Zabriskie died of his wounds ten days later. Several captured Muskrats were eventually shipped to Andersonville, the most detested Confederate prisoner-of-war camp.

General Heckman was among the Union officers captured. He was replaced by Brigadier General George Jerrison Stannard, a New Englander who had proved himself at First Bull Run and went on to help insure the failure of Pickett's Charge at Gettysburg by ordering his Vermont brigade forward to decimate Pickett's right flank.

In the days that followed, Beauregard failed in a feeble effort to evict the Federals from Bermuda Hundred and refused to exchange General Heckman for a Confederate of equal rank. This drew the praise of the *Richmond Examiner* that expressed "a lively satisfaction at the destruction (sic) of Heckman's Brigade and the capture of his daring commander. His celebrated New Jersey Rifle Regiment has been completely destroyed—thus ridding, although at a late date, the bleeding Carolinas of a terrible scourge."

The *Examiner*, in fact, could not have been more wrong. Many of the wounded returned to the 9th New Jersey ranks or were promptly replaced, as were those few Muskrats who had been captured. True enough, training the recruits and conscripts who replaced the veterans took time, but in the interim, the 9th New Jersey was well manned and equipped enough for more action, some of which was especially hazardous.

Sunday, May 22, found Confederate general Beauregard's forces so weakened that Federal forces easily conduct reconnaissance behind enemy lines. Men willing to perform such missions earned five hundred dollars, nearly eight thousand dollars in 2018. Four Muskrats took the challenge but two were captured and examined by General Beauregard himself before spending the rest of the war at Andersonville. Two others successfully returned to the Union lines, but only one carried sufficiently important intelligence to earn the five-hundred-dollar reward.

May 28 brought new orders for the Muskrats, who departed Bermuda Hundred for City Point, Virginia, where they boarded two Fort Monroe–bound transport vessels. Delayed when one of the transports ran aground on May 29, the 9th New Jersey finally reached Cold Harbor, their final ordered destination on the afternoon of June 3. There they found abundant evidence of a Confederate slaughter inflicted by Meade's army, which denied food and water to dozens of wounded Southern men trapped between the Federal and Confederate lines.

The Muskrats entered the fray on June 3 just before noon, targeted almost immediately by Confederate sharpshooting and artillery shells. Sergeant Amos H. Evans later wrote that the 9th New Jersey was "ordered to lie down for we were exposed to a severe fire [*sic*] . . . with no protection but such as we could throw up with cups, plates & hands." The 9th only avoided destruction by constructing small breastworks and digging trenches. In some parts of the battlefield, the Union and Rebel lines were only twenty yards apart. The 9th quickly sustained thirty-five casualties including five dead or mortally wounded before returning to the Bermuda Hundred on June 12.

Eight days later, rumors surfaced that the 9th New Jersey would be sharpshooting again. That very night the regiment moved to the right flank of the Union army at the Petersburg battlefield, cheek to jowl behind the first layer of triple breastworks with the rest of Heckman's old brigade, now supplemented by additional regiments from New York, Pennsylvania, and Maryland.

Within twenty-four hours, the 9th withstood a Rebel attack and did so again two days later. The twenty-fifth brought more Rebels, attacking the left side of the Muskrat position, killing Private Hiram Gray, who had just finished his lunch, remarking that if this was his time at least he would die with a full belly. The Muskrats as a group saw little action after this. Most were posted to Greensboro, North Carolina. Discharges began on June 5.

July 5, 1865, brought a telegram to Greensboro, North Carolina, notifying the 9th New Jersey elements remaining in North Carolina that they would be mustered out of service in about a week. They returned to New Jersey in what Corporal Henry Keenan called "the most rickety [train] cars I ever saw." Praise for the Muskrats soon began to pour in. General S. J. Carter, the district commander, wrote, "I cannot have you leave for home without joining my testimony to those [*sic*] of others, as to the discipline, drill, gallant conduct, soldierly bearing and efficiency of your noble regiment. On the march, in camp, under fire and in the performance of all duties of a soldier, the example of the 9th New Jersey Volunteer Veteran Infantry has been worthy of invitation and entitles it to all praise and commendation."

CHAPTER SIX

The Best He Had

THE BROAD-NOSED COUNTRY BOY FROM MIDDLE TENNESSEE WITH intense eyes and serious demeanor, himself the grandson of a Yankee deserter, is seldom remembered much less mentioned today. Yet his name was once on every mind and many tongues. He was only one of many heroes in the Argonne Forest battles of World War I, but any discussion worth having of sharpshooters, the historic predecessors, and brethren of the modern-day sniper must include Alvin C. York.

He came from the Upper Cumberland Valley, a place in Appalachia with more than its share of legends and lore about frontier fights with Indians and Civil War bushwhackers. This was a place where both Daniel Boone and David Crockett had lived for a time, and generations of inhabitants never forgot it. Fentress County, Tennessee, was remote enough to scarcely even be mentioned, much less visited by state authorities in Nashville and the Federals in Washington, DC. This made Fentress County and much of the Cumberland Valley ideal shadow lands for bootleggers, gun runners, and like-minded criminals of all kinds.

Alvin York was a middle child in a family of eleven children living on a hardscrabble farm, only ten miles from Jamestown, the biggest town in the county, and its seat. Born in mid-December 1887, Alvin saw more than his share of poverty and affliction. Everyone in the York family worked from an early age because there was no other choice. They lived in a one-room cabin near the village of Pall Mall surrounded by seventy-five acres of rocky soil that barely gave them a decent annual corn crop. His father William ran a blacksmith shop from a cave as a side business. Like most settlers in that place and time, the York family hunted for food not as a sport. Young Alvin went hunting with his father for as long as he could remember. And in this way Alvin learned the finer skills of hunting, not to mention when and where to hunt the York table favorites, as coarse as those favorites might sound to the modern ear. "We hunted the red and gray foxes in the daytime and skunks, possums and coons at night," Alvin later recalled.

Alvin also learned to move unseen through the Cumberland Mountains, how to train the few hunting dogs they could afford, and how to track animals. Better yet, Alvin could easily read the weather and decide whether to hunt or blacksmith.

Soon the guns themselves absorbed much of Alvin's interest. He learned to fire a pistol competently but concentrated on the rifles used to bring down squirrels, wild turkey, foxes, and raccoons. Most important of all, those trips gave Alvin time to bond with his father away from the other ten children. William York spent most evenings blacksmithing just to make ends meet. Young Alvin often helped him.

William built a reputation in his part of the Cumberland, winning shooting matches for beef and turkey. The local shooting competitions, often watched by an audience, featured five matches at the conclusion of which the best five shooters each took home a fifth of the freshly slaughtered meat. Alvin later claimed that his father would often bring home the entire cow at the end of such matches.

Turkey shoots were structured differently, with the live target tied to a log at a distance of sixty yards. Each contestant paid a fee for each shot, the objective being to shoot the turkey in head and take it home. According to Alvin York, his father was so good at this sport that he was usually placed at the bottom of the shooting order. This gave the promoter the opportunity to raise enough money to make the contest worthwhile before William took home the prize, or so the story goes, according to Douglas V. Mastriano, whose biography *Alvin York: A New Biography of the Hero of Argonne* is largely relied upon for this chapter. The weapon of choice to these poor farmers was the muzzle-loaded rifle rather than breech-loaded models of more recent vintage.

York recalled years later being inspired by stories of the James-Younger gang and as a consequence becoming an expert with a pistol. "I could take that old pistol and knock off a lizard's or a squirrel's head from that far off [*sic*] that you could scarcely see it." Or so the story goes.

William York was a religious man with a county wide reputation for fairness in arbitrating or advising on conflicts between neighbors that he earned the moniker "Judge York" despite having little or no education at all. 1911 brought new responsibilities for twenty-four-year-old Alvin, whose father was kicked in the head while shoeing a mule that year and died from complications. Since his older brothers had moved away to their own farms by then, Alvin now became responsible for the farm and blacksmithing shop. Perhaps to relieve the tensions of dealing with his new responsibilities, Alvin now began to drink at hell holes called "Blind Tigers" literally located on the Tennessee–Kentucky line. He began hanging out with men who spent their time playing cards and fighting, sometimes with knives. Some three years after his father's death, he had already been arrested and charged with illegally carrying firearms over county lines and killing a turkey flock while intoxicated. This didn't help his case with Frank Asbury Williams, a devout Christian across the small meandering creek called Butterfly Branch from the York place, whose daughter Gracie Loretta had captured Alvin's attention. Not only was Alvin too old for Gracie, Williams didn't want his daughters seeing drunkards, gamblers, and, worst of all, unbelievers.

During a revival service at the nearby Pall Mall Methodist Church on New Year's Day 1915, twenty-eight-year-old Alvin C. York became a Christian. After about a year, he joined the new church in town, the Pall Mall Church of Christ in Christian Union (CCCU), not to be confused with the Christian Church (Disciples of Christ). York became so ardent that he sometimes preached sermons when the regular pastor was called away from his flock. Coincidentally, Gracie Williams and her family also soon joined the CCCU.

Despite these changes, Frank Williams still refused York permission to court Gracie. After all, York was only a "patch" farmer, barely making a living from blacksmithing and raising corn. Gracie accepted Alvin's marriage proposal anyway in June 1917, but a red draft registration card in the mail quickly interrupted the holiday mood along Butterfly Branch. Pastor Pile recommended that Alvin register as the law required but request conscientious objector exemption status. The draft board considered Alvin's notation "Don't want to fight" inadequate and directed him to report for a physical, which he passed. Next, the Fentress County draft board helped Alvin file a "US Form 153," which stated in part that he was "a member of a well recognized sect or organization, organized and existing May 18, 1917, whose existing creed or principles forbade its members to participate in war in any form." The draft board rejected this request, stating that the CCCU was not a well-recognized sect. After the Tennessee State Draft Board rejected two appeals, he reported for military service as directed in mid-November 2017. He reported to Camp Gordon, Georgia. He completed three months of basic training and then reported to Company G, 328th Infantry Regiment, 167th Brigade 82nd Division, also located at Camp Gordon, in early February 2018 for fifteen months of training and duty with other native-born Americans as well as significant numbers of Italian, Slavic, Russian, Greek, and Armenian immigrants. York's company and battalion commanders, E. C. B. Danforth and Major G. Edward Buxton were both Harvard graduates. M1917 US Enfield "Eddystone" rifles were issued to his regiment that March. Few of his classmates had Alvin's experience with rifles; most laughed when he skillfully whetted his front site to reduce glare before firing.

Receiving this weapon that March brought back his reservations about being in combat. After a brief conversation that March with Captain Danforth, his commanding officer, Battalion Commander Buxton welcomed into his office for an informal Christian-to-Christian discussion of York's reservations about fighting, each citing specific passages of the New Testament, which seemed to support their respective positions. After a few minutes of this, Buxton transitioned the conversation into Augustine's Just War arguments and the specifics of German aggression. Captain Danforth joined the conversation with an Old Testament reference that supported Augustine, thus administering the coup de grâce, as it were, to Alvin's case for Christian pacifism.

After a parade reviewed by the governor of Georgia and the widow of Confederate general John Brown Gordon, for whom the camp was named, the 82nd Division began preparations for deployment to France. They traveled by train to Chamblee, Georgia, then on to Camp Upton, New York, after receiving a tumultuous welcome in New York City, less than half an hour away. Many modern readers will be surprised to learn that a significant number of Division men hailing from the Mid-Atlantic area and New England who had not seen their families for over six months left the Camp without permission. Most of these men returned to Camp Upton eventually, but several hundred arrived after the regiment had shipped out for France, only to be placed on later ships. For reasons that remain unclear, York's own regiment traveled by train to Boston, where they boarded two Canadian ships that then sailed for New York City, only a short distance away from Camp Upton where the regiment started. The *SS Scandinavian* and the *SS Grampian* began the voyage across the Atlantic in early May 1918, traversed dangerous waters near Ireland where German U-boats operated, and arrived at Liverpool, England, on May 16. From there they railroaded to Southampton for the short trip across the English Channel to France. They arrived in Le Havre in late May. Just after marching past thousands of waving, cheering French, they stared at a train full of battlefield casualties.

After extensive training in the use of gas masks and other battlefield tactics, the regiment deployed to Amiens near the British Fifth Army. Time was running out for the Germans, or so it seemed to their Supreme Command, which issued the orders to launch Operation Michael in late March. The German initiative nearly destroyed the British Fifth Army, which was fortified some eight weeks later by American regiments. Despite this initiative, President Wilson, General John J. Pershing, and the rest of the military leadership were committed to deploying an independent American army in France.

That said, the Americans in France needed more British training. The 66th (2nd East Lancashire) British Division trained York and the rest of the 328th Regiment in the use of their new British .303 Lee-Enfield rifles. This was necessary, since the British had no .30-06 ammunition for the M1917 rifles that the Americans received back at Camp Gordon.

York and the rest of his regiment left Le Havre on May 22, bound for a place called Eu in the Somme River Valley for a hike twelve miles south into the countryside for quarters in villages around the regimental headquarters at Horcelaines.

While billeted in Floraville, York and his company were trained in the use of Lewis light machine guns, hand grenades and bayonets, mortars, and defensive tactics. The regiment also rotated through front-line British trenches. After inspections by the British Expeditionary Force commander Field Marshal Douglas Haig, John J. Pershing, of rural Laclede County, Missouri, overall commander of the American Expeditionary Forces, visited York's regiment. Soon division orders arrived. They would leave on June 16 for the French XXXII Corps sector east of Verdun, which now would become American. York and the others turned in their British weapons but kept their Empire-issued helmets and gas masks. Now they carried American M1917 Eddystone rifles again as they boarded French trains for the two-day journey to Toul, in the Lorraine. While there he watched some men from his regiment turn a local café into "a No Man's Land." For the most part, however, York read his Bible while others partied.

The 82nd Division now received orders on June 26 for front line service at Rambucourt, a village in a so-called "quiet sector" east of Verdun that had not seen any heavy fighting during the past three years. The 82nd was squeezed into place next to the French 154th Division, which, unlike the 82nd, boasted its own artillery support. The order of battle called for each American regiment to occupy part of the front line, with one battalion directly in front of the Germans, a second supporting regiment about two miles behind them, and a 3rd, six miles or so behind the front trenches in reserve. Earlier, the New England National Guard's 26th "Yankee" Division defended this area for several months.

York's battalion squeezed into the forward trenches among other allied forces practically cheek to jowl with the German enemy, across a no-man's-land that might have been as narrow as ten yards. The opposing forces here were so close together that movement of any kind, even at night, might bring artillery and gas attacks initiated by "the Hun." The trenches themselves were hardly habitable, often knee-deep in putrid rainwater. One observer described the landscape as a largely unbroken "moonlike" vista, broken only by the ruins of the Xivray-et-Marvoisin commune (village) whose "shattered walls made a fine hiding place for the Boche [Germans], both real and imaginary."

Duty here was hardly monotonous, since mostly false gas attack warnings and moments of terror ducking German sniper attacks punctuated the seemingly endless minutes and hours of simply looking out for the enemy. Patrols through no-man's-land at night were particularly dangerous, since individual soldiers sometimes became lost and had to hide for an entire day before crawling back into their own lines while dodging friendly fire. In rare instances, men were killed or injured because they could not pronounce French passwords.

Over the next two months, York and his regiment gradually gained experience they would need for the rest of the war. Since they didn't see many Germans, some wag among them spread the rumor that a single Boche on the other side operated a dozen machine guns and an artillery battery himself.

Now a corporal, York led an automatic weapon squad on several missions into no-man's-land without injury. His division as a whole was not so lucky. By the time they were relieved in the normal rotation of duty on August 10, the 82nd Division had sustained 374 casualties, most of which resulted from poison gas attacks. York's division soon traveled to Pont-á-Mousson, a vibrant large town of thirty thousand souls conveniently located only a half mile from the front in the Marbache Sector. Unknown to the division, at least officially, they would be supporting the first American army offensive in the war, scheduled for September 12.

York and the rest of the division found Pont-á-Mousson to be a quiet, picturesque place hardly touched at all by the hardships of war, almost as if the Germans and their Allied enemies had an agreement in place to keep the town and the surrounding environs in good order. York himself noted that the town was a kind of "earthly paradise" where the "trees and vines were loaded with grapes and apples *and everything* [*sic*]. The gardens were all kept up nice, with everything kinder [*sic*] ripe and ready, and there was plenty of green grass and shade and cool, clean water. It was most hard [*sic*] for us to imagine that we were still at war."

General Pershing designed the St. Mihiel initiative to lay the foundation for a strategic blow in which the city of Metz would be seized by the Allies. First Pershing had to convince French marshal Ferdinand Foch that this initiative should take place before a broader attack. The compromise which Pershing and Foch agreed upon called for a rapid sixty-mile Pershing force march in preparation for the Meuse-Argonne offensive set to be launched a week later.

Early that September, artillery exchanges occurred with increasing frequency on the front near Pont-á-Mousson, amidst increasing rumors and discussions about the upcoming offensive. The Allies openly discussed the war plan in Paris, even as the Germans in this sector began considering a complete withdrawal from the St. Michiel salient, despite a significant buildup of American forces right in front of them. In the end, the Germans abandoned three solid lines of fortified positions from which they could have defended and arguably even decimated the American forces.

This time the Americans launched their offensive against Norroy on September 12, three days after the German evacuation orders were issued. Almost three thousand American and French artillery pieces swept the German line and reserve forces in support of the attack. York later recalled, "It . . . opened with a most awful barrage from our big guns. It made the air and the ground shake. At times you couldn't hear your own voice . . . The air was full of airplanes, most of them American."

York's battalion launched two attacks that first day to keep in contact with the enemy at all times and, more specifically, to seize a German stronghold at Maison Gauthier on the west bank of the Moselle River. The second day York and the rest of the battalion quickly jumped up from their protected trenches, rushed forward through no-man's-land, cutting and climbing through wire, walking or crawling around putrid craters, avoiding German small arms fire and machine guns. York tried to lead his machine gun squad but according to him, the city boys fired wildly once they came into contact with the Germans, burning up ammunition. Still and all, York gave them credit. "They kept on going just the same; they were so full of fight wild cats sure would have backed away from. They wanted to push right on and not stop until they got to Berlin. They cussed the Germans out for not standing and kept yelling at them to wait and fight it out."

The Huns had a plan in mind. While the Americans swooped down toward the objective, a small village called Norroy, the Germans staged a strategic retreat to a superior position not far to the north. York reported that his battalion didn't lose a single man. Little wonder that, since the Germans were retreating from Norroy as quickly as they could.

During a search and destroy mission conducted after the conquest of Norroy, York's squad captured a German sniper who related that his comrades were about 1.25 miles north of town near Vandieres. The Americans learned that before retreating, the Germans forced all but 17 of the 330 Norroy residents to evacuate the town, as a means of reducing the casualties for which the Germans would be blamed. After the assault, the Americans liberated several barrels of German beer, French wine, and a household from which several thousand Belgium (not French) hares escaped being consumed for lunch, or so the story goes.

Although the German counterattack the American battalion prepared for never materialized, the Hun did launch heavy loads of artillery rounds carrying concentrated gas into the town to keep the Americans from chasing them. This was followed by a German mustard gas attack at noon, which was entirely unsuccessful because the regiment had kept their gas masks on.

These German counteroffensive initiatives intended to keep reinforcements from using the Moselle River Road to reinforce the York's regiment north of Norroy succeeded only in keeping the Yanks from their meals that day. Finally, late on September 13, York and his comrades began making runs to a nearby vineyard full of grapes, despite artillery rounds guided by German observation balloons moored just above them.

The St. Mihiel offensive served its original purpose well, preparing the American forces for the battles ahead, while inflicting some seven thousand casualties on the Germans, who also lost at least 450 artillery pieces. More importantly, about two hundred square miles of France was liberated but at the cost of an equal number of American casualties.

After the 69th French Infantry Division arrived on September 21 to replace York's 82nd Division, the Americans rushed by truck from their first time to bat, as it were, in the Major Leagues. With the Meuse-Argonne Offensive scheduled to begin in five days, York and the others approached the new assignment with great confidence. "The majority of the boys were one hundred percent for General Pershing. As a whole, the Army was back of him, believed in him and would follow him anywhere." That said, York didn't see Pershing again.

Modern military historians compare the "en echelon" strategy employed by the Americans during the September 26, 1918, Meuse-Argonne Offensive to Confederate general Robert E. Lee's strategy on the second day of the Battle of Gettysburg. This tactic employs multiple attacks across a single front to fix the targeted enemy units in place and draw away reserves that might otherwise be employed to repel a second series of attacks.

Despite the Germanic sound and appearance of his surname, Field Marshal Ferdinand Foch was a Frenchman through and through. His grand plan for the Meuse-Argonne Offensive called for the First and 3rd British Armies to attack at Canal du Nord on September 27, the

Belgians to attack the Germans north of Ypres on September 28, and for the grand finale, a Franco-British assault near St. Quentin, the final day, four attacks in all beginning with the Americans on September 26.

General Pershing concurred in principle with this order of battle, calling though it did for the American Expeditionary Force to accomplish the most difficult task, taking on Germany's most accomplished divisions in highly challenging terrain, in circumstances where the Germans would be defending their most vital transportation and communication link: the Sedan-Mezieres rail line. Most certainly, the Germans had to know, as did the Americans, that if they lost the Sedan-Mezieres, their entire military operation in France and Belgium was doomed.

Tactically speaking, the Germans had little margin for error along that part of the Western Front where they faced the Americans, in that the depth of the Teutonic defenses was very shallow, no deeper that eleven miles at Argonne, for example.

York and his regiment began the Meuse-Argonne Offensive with a sixty-two-mile journey by train, continued with a bus convoy hosted by French Vietnamese soldiers after a brief break in Bar le Duc and a welcome by their outgoing division commander William P. Burnham. His replacement, Major General George Duncan, was a handpicked friend and associate of General Pershing who Pershing considered to have the aggressive personality necessary to lead York's divisions onto the unforgiving trenches, artillery holes, and no-man's-lands of the Argonne. Duncan later became deeply involved in the fact-finding, which led to the name Alvin York becoming a household word in the United States.

Initially, York's regiment stayed in reserve south of the Argonne in a camp from which the men could clearly hear the opening barrage of the offensive, knowing that sooner rather than later, their 328th Regiment would be deep in the mud, fighting for their lives. At least, they were not undermanned. The American Expeditionary Force consisted of at least 1.3 million men controlling 101 miles of the battlefront, more than any other Allied nation except France. York and the others spent those last few hours before going into action listening to the regimental band perform as rain poured down, sometimes interrupted by brief periods of sunshine. They experienced several false alarms, before going into action in woods nearby. Perhaps they knew through rumor or whispered intelligence that on average the Americans were now suffering twenty thousand casualties a week even as German ardor for this war was weakening. Late that September, anti-war elements of the Social Democrat party won control of the parliamentary government in Germany and demanded an immediate end to the conflict.

Despite such developments, the 82nd Regiment traveled into the southernmost segment of the Argonne Forest in a three-day journey, which directly exposed them to four years of war debris, some of which had been left by the 28th Division in its recent September 26 attack on German lines. Their drivers had ordered them off the buses near Auzeville with the single word "Fini!" leaving them on the edge of the still largely pristine and green portion of the Argonne Forest, in sharp, dramatic contrast with what they would march through, just yards away from the soothing silence beneath the branches.

Unburied bodies were everywhere since 150,000 Germans soldiers died on this part of the battlefront between 1914 and 1918. York and his regiment found ground with little or no vegetation, earth churned by thousands of artillery rounds, most but not all of which had exploded, craters, nearby woods, which according to York appeared as if a cyclone had swept through them.

They marched north into one of those rare parts of the Argonne that was still pristine. They skirted an extensive enemy bunker complex at Champ Mahaut built for crown prince Wilhelm, commander of the German 5th Army. This was his headquarters when the prince directed and monitored the German assault during the 1916 Battle of Verdun. From there, they marched a stone's throw away from Varennes, the ancient place where King Louis XVI and Queen Marie Antoinette had been captured in 1791 and sent on to their execution two years later.

That Sunday morning, October 6, at 10:00 a.m. Daniel S. Smart, 328th Battalion chaplain, preached his last sermon before being killed in action. Ten hours later, the battalion saddled up for an eight-mile night maneuver climbing in to the Meuse-Argonne Valley, west of high ground within the Argonne Forest now held by the German foe. Roads in the area were nearly impassable, blocked as they were by Allied ambulances, tanks, trucks, and even horses, all targeted from time to time with a great deal of accuracy by nearby Hun artillerists. The regiment passed three hours in a downpour waiting for the 15th Artillery Brigade to drive through the Argonne toward the action singing their favorite tunes led by professional vaudevillians within their ranks. When the marching resumed, the regiment faced gas and artillery attacks as well as flares and "star shells," the latter used by the Germans to illuminate rather than penetrate the battlefield. Heavy rain made the march all the more difficult.

Finally the 82nd received specific marching orders, directing them to outflank the Germans on the eastern slopes of the Argonne Forest on October 7 and thereby relieve the Lost Battalion, then composed of some 590 Americans. The secondary purpose of this attack, at least in theory, was to clear the Germans from the eastern Argonne and thereby stop the Huns from continuously firing into the flank of the stalled Americans making their way up the Meuse Valley. General Duncan, now responsible for implementation of this plan of attack, was concerned about the lack of preparation, enemy intelligence, or planning. Worse still, no effort had been made to coordinate the attack with the 1st and 28th Infantry Division or any other neighboring American units. In summary, York's regiment would "attack alone and blind deep into enemy territory," an approach that would cost the Americans dearly in casualties.

Despite these concerns and reservations, York and the rest of the 328th Regiment were expected to be in position next to the slow, meandering Aire River on or before 5:00 a.m. the morning of October 7. Allied leadership expected them to attack, even as the 1st Battalion, sister to York's 2nd Battalion, would attack through a village called Chatel-Chéhéry and clear the high ground that the Americans identified as Hill 223 and the Germans called Castle Hill. Once that was done, the 1st Battalion would enter the Argonne Forest to sever the North-South Supply Road and the parallel small-scale Decauville Railroad. The American military leadership theorized that these two transportation systems were so important that once they fell, the German Army would be forced to abandon the Argonne.

After several American victories, notably including seizure of Hill 180, which the Germans called Beautiful View Hill near Chatel, York and other men of his 2nd Battalion watched the 1st Battalion advance against Hill 223.

While that battle was in progress, German planes began strafing them even as German artillery began pouring fire onto York's 2nd Battalion, forcing the Americans into craters, surrounded by dead horses, dead soldiers of both armies, as well as destroyed tanks and stretcher after stretcher taking the wounded to distant dressing stations.

Soon the American 1st Battalion stalled under the German pres- sure, prompting American leadership to bring York's 2nd Battalion directly into the action. American Field Order No. 2 received an hour before midnight on October 7 directed York's Battalion to "pass through" what was left of the 1st Battalion at 5:00 a.m. the next morning and resume the attack.

Even as York's commanding officers began planning the details of this operation, the Germans began a night attack forcing the 1st Battalion off of the western half of Hill 223. Worse still, the Germans also reinforced the eastern half of Hill 223, creating a death trap for York and the rest of the 2nd Battalion the next morning.

The American plan for October 8 contemplated a three-pronged advance into the Argonne with York's 2nd Battalion in the center and other units to the left, right, and in reserve. The attack was moved back an hour to assure proper placement of both artillery and ground troops. A ten-minute artillery barrage would precede York's attack on the center, which would also be supported by a machine gun company and a mortar platoon, in view of the disaster on Hill 223 the previous night. In theory, York's battalion would also be supported by fifteen

French tanks crewed by Americans, but as a practical matter, the ground was not suitable to use them.

By three that morning, the sleep-deprived, thoroughly drenched, mud-spattered 2nd Battalion began preparations for the first phase of today's operation: moving through Chatel-Chéhéry, a picturesque village that had survived most of the war without damage before sustaining heavy American fire during the present operation. The whole idea was for York's regiment to pass through what was left of the American forces on Hill 223, using narrow boards laid across the Aire River by American combat engineers, since most of the bridges had been destroyed. Then they would march on up a hill to Chatel-Chéhéry. The Americans crossed the Aire River in the darkness before dawn, but as the Americans began the climb toward the village the Germans called in the artillery. Later, York recalled that while darkness still hung over the Argonne, the Meuse Valley below them was anything but quiet. He remembered tens of thousands of men trucks and horses mingled with machine gun fire and artillery rounds. "We were marching, I might say floundering around in columns of squads. The noises were worse than ever and everybody was shouting through the dark and nobody seemed to be able to hear what anybody else said."

Since the artillery array included poisonous gas, the battalion slowed down long enough to put on their gas masks. Consequently, an artillery round killed an entire American squad before they arrived on Hill 223 just before sunrise. At least, the men thought, an artillery barrage would soften up the Germans before they began the assaulting. However, the artillery barrage they had been promised was not delivered, for reasons that remain unclear. Despite this, the officers of York's battalion launched the attack as scheduled at 6:10 a.m. in two waves moving in parallel with a hundred yards between them. York and the rest crashed into the Germans along the western slope of Castle Hill almost immediately. York remembered, "There were some snipers and German machine guns left there hidden in the brush and in fox holes. And they sniped at us a whole heap. [*sic*] I guess we must have run over the top of some of them too, because a little later on we were getting fire from the rear."

Despite this, the Americans plunged from Hill 223 into the valley on the other side, through a clear, dead space without any trees about a half-mile wide, fully exposing them to enemy fire. In no time, as York recalled, in his own quaint Cumberland Valley dialect, the Germans opened fire "in a storm of bullets. I'm a telling you that there valley was a death trap. It was a triangular shaped valley with steep ridges covered with brush, and swarming with machine guns on all sides." York continued that folksy dialect, "I guess our two waves got about halfway across and then jes [sic] couldn't get no further nohow. The Germans done got us and they done gone us right smart. They jes stopped us in our tracks. Their machine guns were up there on the heights overlooking us and well hidden, and we couldn't tell for certain where the terrible heavy fire was coming from. It most seemed as though it was coming from everywhere."

Things were worse than the men of the 2nd Battalion could even know at this point. A battalion supposed to be supporting them provided no protection at all. This was so since a runner delivering a message for York's unit to attack due northwest instead of due west as was originally planned was killed en route. Thus, the supporting battalion, which did get the message about the change in direction, left York's battalion with both flanks exposed.

Not knowing any of this, York's platoon leader, Lieutenant Kirby Stewart, waved the men forward into the center of the open valley, until a burst of machine gun fire threw him down. Stewart stood back up and plunged forward until a German bullet hit him in the head. York's platoon now stopped on open ground and began digging in, seeing almost immediately that their left flank lay exposed to machine gun fire from a hill above them. Four squad leaders, including York, were ordered to take out those machine guns with seventeen men behind them.

Now, for the first time during this action, the war gods smiled on the Americans as the delayed artillery fire that was supposed to soften up the Germans at 6:00 a.m. now erupted. This forced the Germans with York and the others in their sights to run for cover.

The Americans scrambled five hundred yards up the hill, which had been the objective before the American artillery barrage stopped.

This gave York and the other squad leaders time to plan their next move. Before going into the Argonne, they would flank the Germans in their sector. The Americans marched toward a small stream to do just that, stumbling upon two Germans wearing Red Cross armbands who were filling canteens, as York later recalled, "They jumped out of the brush in front of us and run liked two scared rabbits. We called to them to surrender and one of our boys fired and missed. And they kept a-going [*sic*]. And we kept after them. We wanted to capture them before they gave the alarm. We now knowed [*sic*] by the sounds of the firing that we were somewhere behind the German trench and in the rear of the machine guns that were holding up our big advance [on the big center hill]. We still couldn't see the Germans and they couldn't see us. But we could hear them machine guns shooting something awful."

Six of the seventeen Americans with York had been killed by now; the survivors were spread all across the meadow, just beneath (or so it seemed) a German machine gun that was firing at anything that moved. As the Americans assessed who was dead and who was still alive, York quickly realized that Corporal Murray Savage, his best friend in the army, had been shot to pieces, parts of his body and shreds of his clothing now spread here and there across the meadow.

Seeing this, York now took the initiative. He was the only non-commissioned officer not dead or wounded. He promptly resolved that he would stop the killing, meaning that he would stop any additional Americans from dying if he could. While platoon members provided covering fire, York charged a German machine gun nest, but not directly. Instead, he charged up an adjoining hill, crossed, a German supply road and then took a sniping position just above it. His view from the sniper hide revealed several groups of German soldiers occupying two other roads above and parallel the place from which he was doing his reconnaissance. He was at the very tip of a "V" from which he could see the machine gun crew and supporting riflemen. York killed them all, all nineteen of them, using about forty-six rounds of ammunition, urging the Germans to surrender throughout the entire ambush. The problem was, none of them could have heard York, nor did that matter at all to his American buddies who had just lost so many friends.

York now made a run for it back to the relative safety of the meadow and the survivors in his platoon. Only too late did he realize that a German platoon leader had seen York, ordered some of his men to fix bayonets, and charged out of the German trench with another twelve soldiers. York slid to a halt, pulled out his M1911 Automatic Colt Pistol (ACP) and began picking them off from back to front, just as he did when hunting turkey flocks. Private Beardsley pulled out his own Colt Pistol and helped him. Between them, Beardsley and York killed six of the thirteen men who charged them, bringing York's count for the day to twenty-five dead Germans in all. A German lieutenant named Paul Jurgen Vollmer walked over to York, saying in perfect English, "Good Lord! If you won't shoot anymore I will make them give up." York pointed his pistol at Vollmer and nodded his head. Vollmer was in charge of the 125th Regiment that morning. And as a consequence of Vollmer overestimating the number of Americans he was up against, surrendered a regiment of Germans to a handful of Americans.

Moments later, as York and his prisoners crossed the valley, Lieutenant Joseph A. Woods gaped at the spectacle from a distance, thinking that he would soon be confronted with a counterattack. Soon he noticed that the Germans were unarmed, and was that York at the head of the column? York saluted Lieutenant Woods when he arrived at Hill 223, simply announcing "Company G reports with prisoners, sir." When all had returned to Chatel-Chéhéry, Lieutenant Woods counted 132 German prisoners in all, with the battalion commander, Major James Tillman present to vouch for the count. After the German-American column survived a German artillery barrage, the battalion intelligence officer asked Vollmer a few questions and found the German orders to counterattack and seize Castle Hill from the Americans at 10:30 in Vollmer's pocket.

York's actions, at the very least, cleared the American front and left flank, caused the Germans to abandon some thirty machine guns, and enabled the 2nd Battalion to resume the stalled attack, breaking the German lines permanently.

The German Army elements in the area did not panic, but it was clear that the planned German counterattack to take Castle and Beautiful View hills had been preempted by York's actions. Shortly thereafter, for a variety of reasons, the German Army was ordered to withdraw from the Argonne. The Germans lost more than eighty thousand dead here, but York and his regiment would clash with them one more time before the Germans left Argonne behind.

This is not to say that the Americans suffered minimal casualties in the Argonne. The assault to capture Hill 223 from the Germans the day before York's victory virtually decimated the 1st Battalion of York's 328th Regiment. His own 2nd Battalion suffered its greatest losses in all of World War I on the very day York's actions arguably turned the battle. Most of the damage to York's battalion happened after York marched the 132 German prisoners into the American lines. This resulted from the last German counterattack in this segment of the Argonne, during which the Hun recaptured the village of Cornay, killed dozens of Americans, and captured another one hundred.

York returned from his prisoner march to Varennes on October 9; he told his commanding officer Captain E. C. B. Danforth where he had been and explained exactly how Danforth's company had been able to advance so far. Somewhat stunned, Danforth gave York permission to take some stretcher bearers back to the battlefield to search for survivors, but York didn't find any.

There was very little time to ponder all this, although later York reflected that "there was nothing I could do now for Corporal Murray Savage or any of the other boys that . . . lost their lives." Two men on either side of him had been killed in the action that he just survived. His perspective was that he had been saved by divine intervention.

Whatever his standing with Divine Providence, during the skirmishes that followed that very day, York's regiment tried to advance along the right side of the German supply road but were stopped after only three hundred yards by some of the same Wurttembergers they had been fighting the last two days.

The next day, October 10, as the Germans retreated from the Argonne, York's regiment rested several hours before moving on to the next mission. York's regiment had sustained 718 casualties, including 28 officers. York and others could not know that they would experience more than their share of similar battles in the days before the war came to an end.

Their next target was the so-called Kriemhilde Line, a segment of the German Siegfried (American name Hindenburg) line. The Kriemhilde segment featured bunkers trenches and wires arrayed to channel American soldiers into killing zones. German strong points were fortified by machine guns and artillery. The luck of the draw placed York's regiment on the right flank of the attack near the town of Sommerance confronted by a substantial line of wires and other obstacles.

Monday, October 14, brought an Allied artillery barrage before the 328th Regiment, 1st Battalion led the way into battle at 8:30 a.m. with York's own 2nd Battalion some 550 yards behind them, challenged by small arms fire, and artillery shells, some of which carried poisonous gas. One shell came so close to York and his squad that they were blown into the air. Incredibly, none of them were wounded, much less killed.

Logically enough, the 1st Battalion took the brunt of the initial German attack, struggling through the rolling hills of the Meuse Valley. Much of the 1st was in the midst of cutting its way through the wire barricades when the artillery barrage and machine gun fire began taking a heavy toll. Observation balloons above them made this deadly German targeting almost easy. Somehow the Americans in the center and on the left managed to outflank the Germans and their wire obstacle protections, but the fortunes of war on the right flank were another matter. Once again, York's 2nd Battalion had no protection on its right flank because the 42nd Rainbow Division was delayed and became embattled to the east.

The next phase of the battle for the Kriemhilde found York's 2nd Battalion taking advantage of the hole the 1st Battalion made earlier. This was no picnic to be sure, since their way over the obstacles was made all the more precarious by constant artillery barrage and machine gun fire, made all the more formidable by the shock of seeing dozens, if not hundreds, of dead and wounded men of both sides being treated and retrieved by stretcher bearers and medics. The 2nd Battalion walked past all this as quickly as possible, knowing nothing else could be done. Historians later learned that many of the dead were struck the very second they raised their heads above the fray. Captain Danforth easily assessed the danger ahead of the 2nd Battalion; Germans held the high ground with good visibility of the hill the Americans were about to attack, across an entire half-mile killing zone without a single tree for cover. The 1st Battalion men ahead of them were literally climbing the hill on their bellies, but somehow York's unit pushed on through these slower 1st Battalion men toward the regimental objective they shared: the St. Georges–St. Juvin Road.

Once again the 2nd Battalion was ahead of the pack and once again they paid the price. Since there was no one on their right flank to protect them from German machine gun fire that soon began arriving from three sides, Captain Danforth and Major Tillman pulled the men back to dig in, since the prospects for an immediate German counterattack were high.

While the 1st and 2nd Battalions coped with constant machine gun fire and artillery shelling, deskbound army paperwork artists assessed the severe losses sustained over the past few weeks and consolidated the 1st and 2nd Battalion within the 328th Regiment on October 14 and then combined York's own 328th with the 327th effective the next day. Perhaps not having received word of this consolidation, the 82nd Division headquarters issued orders for an attack across that part of the front theoretically under 82nd Division control on October 15, the very day the merger was to take place.

Artillery fire would be directed at the German positions throughout the late night and early evening of October 14 and 15, supported by an Allied chemical attack on the Germans at 4:00 a.m. Enhanced artillery fire would begin at 7:25 a.m. followed by the advance itself five minutes later. The first objective was a steep ravine locally known as the Ravine aux Pierres at least a half mile from where the newly combined 1st Battalion would begin the charge.

The evening and early morning proceeded as planned, but the Germans ruined the plan with an unexpected 7:00 a.m. artillery barrage, followed fifteen minutes later by a German assault against the prospective American attackers. Unfortunately for the Americans, this was no simple straightforward attack. The Germans lured the Americans out of their foxholes by briefly stopping the artillery barrage and then opened up with machine guns. This tactic combined with a low fog that no doubt had been part of the attack plan meant that gray-clad German soldiers coming toward the Americans a few minutes later were an entire surprise. York and the rest of the men in his combined regiment struggled to hang on despite all this, with limited success; some of the American elements fell back several hundred yards. On the other hand, the German attack presented some of the Americans with new opportunities. When Captain Danforth and Major Tillman realized that somehow the German left flank became exposed, if only momentarily, American infantrymen were rushed in to rake the Hun with rifle fire. Better yet, American light machine gun fire was soon added to the Wagneresque symphony, killing any and all Hun who could not run or be carried away.

Despite these efforts and the advantages the Americans gained in the successful Ravine aux Pierres offensive, at the end of the day, the Germans still held the heavily manned, well-fortified heights above it. The Germans exploited these advantages to drive the Americans back into the very lines and foxholes where they started that morning.

The evening of October 15 brought heavy rain and German machine gun and air attacks from the north and east against the salient (bulge) that York's unit created in the last offensive action. Time seemed to slow almost to a halt as the remaining days of October, and more miserable, rainy weather only added to the sad condition of York's regiment, living day to day as they did in fields of mud dotted by artillery shell holes filled with water. The dreariness was relieved, if only temporarily, by rotations away from the front lines to what was left of Sommerance, where food, bathing facilities, and even new clothing was plentiful, however briefly.

Back on duty, the German artillery and machine gun fire pounded York and his company more than ever, interrupted only by occasional aerial dogfights, which frontline soldiers of both armies watched and enthusiastically cheered. York's 82nd Division was relieved just after midnight in the early morning of November 1, in the very midst of a last, massive Allied offensive. Walking through all of this in the darkness, York and the others no doubt pondered their losses. The 328th Regiment, which had been consolidated with the 327th, or what was left of it, lost 1,189 dead or injured, representing a casualty rate of about 30 percent. York, now promoted to sergeant wrote that "we scarcely seemed the same outfit." Eventually, they were moved to buses and later, on a seven-day leave to Aix les Bains, which had been a bath resort since Roman times. The armistice signed at 5:00 a.m., November 11, became effective six hours later. York could only say that he was ready to go home, but that didn't happen for several months. He attended Christmas dinner with President Wilson, and Mrs. Wilson remained behind to assist with the February 1919 investigation into whether York should receive the Medal of Honor. By the time the ship carrying the 328th Battalion reached Hoboken, New Jersey, on the afternoon of May 22, Alvin York was a national celebrity.

Chapter Seven

Freelance Snipers

AMERICANS FIGHTING IN THE PACIFIC DURING WORLD WAR II quickly learned that the Japanese were masters of concealment and camouflage. Sniping itself? Not so much. Still and all, by the time of the August 1942–February 1943 Guadalcanal conflict in the Solomons, American countermeasures became indispensable, because of situations like that reported by journalist Richard Tregaski, from personal experience on the island of Maranikua, where he found himself entirely exposed to enemy fire one day. According to *Stalk and Kill: The Sniper Experience* by Adrian Gilbert, one of two primary sources for this chapter, he dove for a nearby tree in an area almost entirely free of protecting jungle foliage but soon realized that he was still in a danger zone, quickly confirmed by a round that nearly struck his left shoulder. Jumping into a nearby bush exposed him to hundreds of ants but concealed Tregaski from the Japanese sniper, or so he thought. Once again a Japanese .25 cracked loudly but passed far enough away from Tregaski that he jumped between two trees growing among some pineapple plants. Tregaski had escaped for now but soon ran into yet another Japanese sniper, while watching a dogfight between Japanese Zeroes and American fighters in the sky above Guadalcanal. For no particular reason, he happened to notice some movement in a tree just across from him in a valley. Looking closer, he noticed someone moving his arms and body around in the "crotch" of the tree, where the main limbs came together at the tree trunk. This time, his previous experience with Japanese snipers paid off. "I was so amazed at seeing him so clearly that I might have sat there and reflected on the matter if my reflexes had not been functioning, which they fortunately were. I flopped flat on the ground just as I heard the sniper's gun go off and the bullet whirred over my head." That movement that he noticed? That was the sniper moving the gun into place to kill Tregaski.

He learned that Japanese preferred tree positions, even though the danger of being detected and shot there was high. This was so because killing a single American made the risk worthwhile in the Japanese military culture. A November 1942 US Intelligence bulletin quoted one marine sergeant's experience and summarized what had been learned. Marines reported that they (the Japanese) were concealed in trees, bushes, and buildings. Time and time again, American forces passed through an area and took fire from behind. A second marine officer said that the Japanese use a large number of snipers. "They shot at us from the top of coconut trees, slit trenches, garden hedgerows, from under buildings, from under fallen palm leaves . . . One sniper shot down from a tree, had coconuts strung around his neck." He also remembered, "Another in a palm tree had protected himself with armor plate. Our Thompson [sub-machine-guns] and BARs [Browning Automatic Rifles] proved to be excellent weapons for dealing with snipers hidden in trees."

The Japanese sniping strategy and tactics were easy enough to identify after those first few weeks on Guadalcanal. Their primary objective was killing as many American officers and noncommissioned officers as possible. The Japanese looked for anyone with the tell tale insignia from their hiding places on the flanks and in weapons emplacements. Many Japanese wore green uniforms and sometimes even painted their faces, arms, and hands to match the colors of the vegetation from which they were sniping. Some even donned vegetation held in place by camouflage netting.

The first monthly *Marine Corps Gazette* published in 1945 focused on jungle warfare strategy and the advantages potentially available to any sniper while conducting jungle warfare. "There are certain advantages in jungle warfare which are invariably entered on the black side of the defender's combat ledger. The defender is usually able to select the position he will defend, dig in, get his supplies, [sight] and camouflage his weapons, conceal his personnel, establish his security and wait for the attacker, all according to a previously prepared plan." The *Gazette* acknowledged that "the attacker is burdened with the problem of locating the defender, feeling out the position, and blasting his way through it. In the process of doing so, he cannot expect to employ cover and concealment as effectively as the defender because he must move. In moving, he must expose his personnel. Thus, the well-concealed enemy sniper is automatically provided with an abundance of targets without exposing himself."

Next, the *Gazette* focused on the weapons the Japanese typically used, commenting on their tendency in late 1944 to use .30 (caliber) small arms in an effort to secure penetration and "brush cutting" qualities. The *Gazette* noted that "the majority of [Japanese] soldiers and practically all snipers still use .25 caliber weapons. Snipers are usually equipped with rifles, carbines or Nambu light machine-guns" before getting down to specifics. "The .25 [caliber] weapon will not cut brush or penetrate like a .30 [caliber] weapon. It will, however, penetrate our helmet (sic) at ranges of 150 yards or more. This is penetration enough in most cases. Its most annoying characteristic is that for all practical purposes the Japanese small-arms powder is usually smokeless and generates little muzzle blast when used in a .25 weapon. Thus a sniper can 'hole up' or 'tree up' with any of his three small arms, and although he may fire considerably, we will seldom, if ever, locate him by smoke or muzzle blast."

Finally, the article focused on a fundamental problem facing the Americans during the remaining months of the war in the Pacific. "At the beginning of the hostilities [in the Pacific] and in many cases even now the [Japanese] was generally a better woodsman than our Marines. He was meticulously trained and equipped for jungle warfare long before Pearl Harbor and he had received the training and used the equipment in the jungle. The training had been realistic and tough. Jungle techniques had been developed and proven while we were parading in blues at the Marine Corps Base. The [Japanese] sniper had learned to live successfully as an animal in the jungle; while our boys were enjoying a standard of living they had been raised to regard as a right, rather than a privilege."

One incident that Tregaskis personally watched during the fight for Guadalcanal brought these problems of strategy and tactics home. When a Japanese soldier quietly snuck past three American tanks and a platoon of American Infantry, all missed him. "The [Japanese soldier] continued to run. He was headed for the beach. All along our front line, rifles banged and machine guns clattered; the tracers arched around the running [Japanese soldier]. Then he sank into the underbrush, took cover and Colonel Pollock shouted: 'Don't shoot; you might hit our own tanks.'"

Incredibly, Tregaskis recalled the Japanese soldier "jumped up and ran another forty or fifty feet towards the shore, then sank into cover again." Despite the warning, several shots were fired at him. As usual, each marine was eager to do the job, so Captain Sherman brought some order to the scene. "One man fire," Sherman shouted. "He designated a grizzled, leather-faced Marine to do the shooting. I noticed that the man wore the chamois elbow pad and fingerless gloving of a rifle marksman. The Marines told me he was Gunnery Sergeant Charles E. Angus (of Nashville, Tennessee) a distinguished marksman who had won many a match in the states."

Tregaskis remembered watching Sergeant Angus "as if he were the spotlight of a play, when the [Japanese soldier] jumped up again and began to run. Angus was nervous. He fired several shots, working his bolt fast and missed. He inserted another clip of cartridges, fired one of them, but the [Japanese soldier] had sunk down into cover again."

Tregaskis remembered some disappointment, but not for long. The Japanese soldier "flopped on the beach." He was evidently heading for the sanctuary of the water, hoping to swim for it. But now he started to get up again, and that was as far as he got. He had only reached a crouch when Sergeant Angus, now quite calm, took careful aim and let one go. Now the Japanese soldier dropped as "if the ground had been jerked out from under him. It was a neat shot–at about two hundred yards."

An Australian artilleryman named Russell Braddon had one experience dealing with a Japanese sniper hiding at the very top of a tree that might have even been funny had it not been deadly serious. He was "amazed to see a fellow gunner raise a heavy [.55 caliber] Boyes anti-tank rifle to his shoulder, aim high and fire. He was at once flung backwards, while the half-inch shell most certainly passed harmlessly into the stratosphere." By the time Braddon reached him, "he was rubbing his shattered right shoulder and swearing softly with that consummate fluency which is the prerogative of the Australian farmer. What the hell are you trying to do, Harry?" I asked. "Get that bloody sniper up the top of that bloody tree," he replied, tersely. Braddon now realized that the "Boyes rifle had not sufficient elevation to hit a tree high up." However, since the sniper fired from behind the top of the tree trunk, he could be shot through it; a Boyes rifle was therefore essential for the job. Now Braddon suggested that the rifle be fired with the barrel resting on his own shoulder. "Harry took a long aim, apparently quite undeterred by the bursts of bullets from all sides, which our stance attracted. I was not in the least undeterred. In fact, as we stood there, our feet spread wide apart to take some of the shock, I was very deterred indeed. Then Harry fired and I was crushed to the ground and Harry was flung against a tree and the sniper toppled gracelessly out from behind his tree, thudding on to the earth below, and our job was done."

One battalion of the 163rd Infantry 41st Division in New Guinea developed another more elaborate anti-sniper strategy in January 1943, as described later by a historian, who recalled that "beneath the eyes of these [Japanese] killers, life quickly became not worth living unless we could shoot them out of their trees. Grimly the Musket garrison . . . developed a system of counter-sniping." Their strategy for dealing with such problems featured three steps. "First we had to deal with the most immediate threat from [Japanese] Perimeters Q-R which lurked in holes 20–30 yards before us. We set up two-man counter-sniper teams in slit trenches on the forward edge of [the] Musket perimeter. Then while one of the other men searched through the jungle (with field glasses if he had them) the other man cuddled his well-cleaned rifle and waited. When the [Japanese] shots rang out, the observer carefully spotted the green area where the shots came from. He pointed out the direction of the fire, let the rifleman observe through his glasses. Then the rifleman fired until the Jap was silent, or Jap fire retaliated close enough to make him lie prone. Thus we secured our forward area."

The second step in this strategy relied on counter-sniping teams placed on the flank and to the rear of the perimeter, relying on home-made ladders made of telephone wire for tree-climbing. "Once the two-man tree teams were aloft, we got to work. We shot at all trees which seemed to harbor [Japanese] rifles. When [Japanese] fired, we followed our standing order. All teams returned fire. If unsure of the actual target, we engaged probable [Japanese] trees in the general direction of the popping fire. With our M-1 and 1903 rifles, we shot at 200–300 yards."

Since these measures alone didn't take care of the problem, the historian recalled, "As soon as we posted sniper teams in trees, we could take the offensive. We could use these teams to guide attack patrols on the ground. We sent out small foot patrols of two or three men. Under direction from tree observers, our patrols shot down snipers or slashed other targets on the flanks."

Later, as a fourth step, when 37 mm guns became available, the 163rd "topped" the trees where Japanese snipers were suspected of hiding. This approach was at variance with the more common "one-on-one" strategy of locating and then disposing of individual snipers.

One marine later recalled using the more tradition approach in Saipan, the next year. "We were pinned down on the beach at Saipan by a machine-gun bunker. The pill-box commanded a sweeping view of the area, and there was just no way we could get at it. Plenty of our boys died trying." Eventually, he recalled "one of our ninety-day wonders got on the horn and requested a sniper. A few minutes later, I saw two old gunnery sergeants sashaying towards us, wearing shooting jackets and campaign hats! As soon as I saw these Smokey Bears bobbing over to us, I figured this could be some show. And it was."

First, the veteran sergeants "skinnied up to the lieutenant and just asked him to point out the bunker. Then they unfolded two shooting mats, took off their Smokey Bears [hats] and settled down to business. One manned a spotter's scope while the other fired a 1903 Springfield with a telescopic sight rig."

The marine estimated that the bunker was 1,100 or 1,200 yards away, "but in just a few minutes, with three or four spotting rounds, this old gunny on the Springfield slipped a round right into the bunker's firing slit. One dead machine-gunner. But their commander just struck another man on that gun. Our sniper shot him too." The marine recalled that "after the fourth man bit a slug, I think they [the Japanese] got the idea. We moved up on their flank and destroyed the bunker while our snipers kept the machine-gun silent. Then the two gunnies dusted themselves off, rolled up their mats and settled their Smokey Bears back on their heads. And just moseyed away."

John Fulcher stood nearly six feet tall and had his father's light-colored eyes. Through his whole life, it was his Cherokee mother's black hair and copper skin that caught people's attention most of the time. So it was at Camp Bowie, Texas, in the early fall of 1942 when the drill sergeant asked if he had ever scalped anyone. John had a stock answer for that: not yet. During boot camp for the 36th Division of the Texas National Guard he told the grizzled old non-commisioned officer (NCO) that he had signed up to kill some Germans and Japanese. Now, after basic training was over, that same sergeant was looking for snipers.

Somebody in the back ranks said that snipers didn't have much of a life expectancy, but that didn't keep John Fulcher and a few others from volunteering. It was all convenient enough, since the sniper school was right there at Fort Bowie.

Before he knew it, John was trying to clean oily Cosmoline rust inhibitor off of his own brand new M-1D rifle. His weapon was much like other M-1s except for the heavy barrel, custom trigger action, flash suppressor, and a telescopic sight that came in mighty handy shooting at targets five hundred yards away for practice.

The army "scout/snipers" would typically operate in six- or twelve-man squads, out ahead of everybody else in no-man's-land or sometimes even behind enemy lines. The primary scouting objective was learning what the enemy was doing and maybe even planning to do. The other part of the job was officially called "skirmishing," picking off any enemy they could find, using the skills of a sniper, according to the treatise *One Shot, One Kill* by C. W. Sasser and C. Roberts.

The 36th Division landed at Salerno, Sicily, on Wednesday, September 8, 1943. The Italian army there had surrendered but not the Germans. Fulcher and the rest of snipers watched the invasion from the ship rails until they were directed onshore with the headquarters troops for their first assignment, dropping German officers wherever they could be found during the push to Rome. The basic idea was to find a ridge or a hilltop and look for an officer or someone else if an officer wasn't available to kill *with a single shot*. Fulcher said later that most of the men he shot dropped "like a sack of rotten potatoes."

Like the rest of the snipers, Fulcher asked himself time and time again what he would do the first time he had a German in his sights. Fulcher later recalled how one bright, clear morning he had gone his own way into "the bush" wriggled into a well-concealed hiding place (called a hide) at the top of a hill above a narrow, brown valley traversed by a dry stream bed, expecting to find German targets on the hill opposite his position. Sooner than he expected, Fulcher spotted a German patrol of five or six soldiers cutting their way through brush on the hill opposite his position. Since they were about seven hundred yards away, he let them pass, hoping for closer targets.

Soon one appeared in his scope as the birds fluttered above Fulcher. Long before he expected, a young German moving through the bushes about one hundred yards away captured his attention. The Hun was relieving himself in the bushes when Fulcher missed his first shot and was running for his life when Fulcher missed him a second time. Fulcher vowed that wouldn't happen again.

Fulcher's second time out was with other snipers, who found a dirt road traveled by the Germans and divided surveillance among several two-man teams, each consisting of a spotter and a shooter. Fulcher himself found a hide with a great escape route amidst a jumble of boulders on the side of a ridge above the road the snipers were watching. Weather and light conditions were perfect. Sunrise brought an entire company of Germans newbies in freshly starched gray and green uniforms marching in formation. Small clouds of dust rose behind them as they walked along. Fulcher looked at the sweating brow of an officer that he took to be the commander, made a quick internal calculation, and nodded to his partner. Game on.

This time there was no hesitation, only the cool deliberation with which Fulcher had killed his first deer. This time the commanding officer looked surprised as he fell to a sitting position on the road, soon falling onto his back, as dead as he could ever be. His men scattered into drainage ditches and even shell craters as fast as their legs would carry them. Some looked out from their hidey holes, giving Fulcher at least three targets, none of which he took, for worry that taking those shots would reveal his hide. Fulcher's partner took out one of the enlisted men. Fulcher later recalled, "After I killed the officer in the road, I felt something inside me begin to change. When you go into combat you revert to the most vicious kind of animal that ever walked the earth. You become a predator. I got to where it hurt me more to kill a good dog than a human being."

Fulcher soon made sergeant and became a sniper squad leader. As the American offensive continued, he noticed that "whenever the desperate Germans fell back from a position they left their own snipers behind as rear guards. They hid in the bombed-out towns and waited for the Allies to come. Kraut artillery bracketed the open places, while the German snipers hid to cover places the artillery couldn't reach. You got mortared and ran for cover, only to find some jerry sharpshooters plinking at you. The German snipers tool a toll of their own against the Allies."

One observer of this battle remarked that "it took a sniper to root out a sniper. Our experience in the trade helped us locate where the enemy marksmen might be hiding in old churches or in the ground-work maze of bombed out buildings. Before our troops went in, they called up the snipers and we went over the rubble foot by foot with binoculars."

From time to time during the American offensive, Fulcher recalled, it became sniper against sniper. "Dog-tired and footsore, my company on point for the battalion wended its way into one of those countless, nameless towns we encountered on the way to Rome. It had been gutted by shellfire; the point men blazed a pathway around piles of brick and collapsed frameworks and broken glass." Fulcher's own squad "was holding down a place with the headquarters element toward the rear of the formation when a shot echoed ahead in the ruins. From where I was, all I could see was the backs of GIs as they ducked behind parts of walls and buildings crouching there and not moving. The company commander went scurrying to the front, followed by his radio man. I always looked for that antenna when I was deciding which enemy to shoot."

Fulcher soon heard two more shots but held his men in a protected spot until a runner slid in next to him. The German sniper had killed three Americans and the commanding officer (CO) wanted to see Fulcher about solving this problem that is if Fulcher could find the commander without getting shot himself. "I tapped the sniper next to me for a spotter. The runner stayed behind with his head down while my spotter and I dodged forward from building to building until we reached the commander crouching behind the remains of a house. He was breathing heavily and sweat had matted plaster dust on his face."

"We don't know where the hell the bastard is out there," the CO said. Fulcher went for a look, crawling to the end of the building. "I had learned to memorize every detail of terrain after one quick peek. I took that peek from right next to the ground, past some kind of bottle half-filled with spoiled food."

The situation was hardly simple, Fulcher recalled. "To my front was a street that ran away from me to where it intersected another street filled with debris from a recent shelling. A bed with the mattress still on it rested atop a pile of concrete wreckage. One of the dead GIs lay at the intersection. He seemed so much a part of the general waste that you hardly noticed him."

Fulcher used that dead GI to calculate roughly where he could find the German sniper. "I figured the sniper's hide to be farther down the street where he could control both it and the intersection."

Fulcher had a plan in mind. The general idea was to give the German sniper a target and see if he could be coaxed into showing himself: "We had used the trick before. My spotter crawled down to the end of the wall nearest the street while I eased my M-1 through a crack clogged with enough ivy to camouflage my movements." Then, as Fulcher watched the terrain through his scope, his spotter pulled out a stick, put his own helmet on it, and slowly dangled it above the wall. "He jerked it back down and waited a minute or two before revealing it again. This time the sniper was ready . . . An 8-millimeter German bullet drilled the helmet and sent it spinning." Fulcher saw some movement through his scope. "A thin puff of smoke popped from the window of a building about a hundred yards down the street. There wasn't much left of the building, but it still had enough roof over its remaining window to hold shadows inside."

Fulcher held his fire to avoid spooking the German sniper. He compared this to hunting a squirrel that ran to hide in its hole. "All you had to do was sit down and wait. Sooner or later curiosity overcame caution and the squirrel stuck its head out again. I kept my scope centered on the window, waiting." Fulcher's rule was that he would never shoot more than two or three times from the same hide. "I was counting on this German being careless or lazy," Fulcher recalled later.

Fulcher remembered every detail as he told the story years later, right down to the overcast weather and the inside of the house he used as a hide. Before long, he noticed the quick but unmistakable glint of a rifle barrel, followed by the outline of the sniper peeking out of his hide. Almost like a squirrel.

He fired and watched as "an invisible rope yanked the German's weapon from his hands and hurled it into the street. The German's body lunged forward across the window sill where it hung head down, his hands fluttering a moment against the street." Fulcher watched the body convulse a few more times while a dark pool of blood gathered below its head. Then everything was still. Fulcher later recalled that "I was scalping the dead German when a green lieutenant who had just hooked up with the outfit came up to see what was happening.

He turned to the paleness of a West Texas sky in the middle of summer."

———

The armorer at Fort Dix had a sly grin on his face after putting a brand new bolt-action .30-caliber 1903 Springfield rifle in the hands of William E. Jones, a brand-new private who had just fired the highest score of any enlisted man in his company. Having that rifle in his hands told everyone in the 8th Infantry Regiment, Fourth Division, that once they were overseas, Jones would be *the* sniper for Company I.

Jones had grown up in Tennessee depending on squirrel, rabbit, and possum hunting for food on the table. And when his division went ashore at Normandy on June 6, 1944, Company I spearheaded the operation. Fortunately, the division didn't meet as much opposition as other Americans on the beach confronted that day. Once they were off the beach, they found "a patchwork quilt of little fields enclosed by hedges of hawthorn, brambles and vines tangled together to make walls ten to fifteen feet tall."

He couldn't help but notice the shallow graves topped with makeshift crosses, or, just as often, a soldier's rifle pushed muzzle down into the mud, sometimes with a helmet on top, sometimes not. From Jones's perspective, this was no surprise since this seemed to Jones to be perfect ambush country.

Writing later, he recalled wooden platforms in the trees filled with Germans snipers using flashless gunpowder that made them almost impossible to spot. The platforms above the roads and paths that didn't have embedded snipers had machine guns instead.

None of this kept Jones from continuously cleaning his rifle with the small oil can, cleaning rod, and bore patches that he kept in his pack with old socks, underwear, and C rations. There wasn't any choice about this since he had discovered that without frequent cleaning, the critical insides of an M-1 rifle would soon turn to rust. His daily routine included laying out the weapon on a spread out pouch, checking for and eliminating rust, and putting oil on the stock, since there was no wax available in the hedgerows.

Dealing with German snipers became routine for Jones. A single shot would ring out; someone would call for a medic, before calling for Jones, who now had to low-crawl through yards of brambles while keeping his rifle out of the mud. Sometimes, this all started with more than a single German rifle shot. One particular day reminded Jones of springtime in the Smoky Mountains, until he realized that those meadowlarks he heard weren't really birds but a German machine gun:

"I slithered down a little gully and worked my way up to another sergeant lying in a depression with his helmet off and the sun shining on red hair. He looked at me and gave a thin smile, then looked back across an open field of short new grass that abutted a hedgerow about three hundred yards away." Jones recalled that "a low hill rose beyond it, on top of which perched an old farmhouse. The empty windows did not reflect the sunlight. The panes were gone, shot out probably."

Jones knew how careful he had to be, if he were to survive. "I kept my head low while I started to scan the hedgerows through my scope. The German sniper was no slouch. He had already picked off two of our boys. I heard a medic over in the bushes working on one of them."

Jones gathered what information he could from the men working on an American who had been shot through the lung. A sergeant in the group thought that the German shot might have come from their right flank.

Jones surveyed the situation himself. "I detected a large knot high in the top of a tree. I studied it a second and was about to slide on past, thinking it [was] a deformity in the tree, when it moved." Jones stared at it for a minute or two and finally concluded that it must have been a bird. Then he moved his scoped slowly down the hedgerow, hoping against hope that the sniper would be careless enough to reveal himself. Then he took a second look at something that caught his attention briefly moments before. "I returned to the knot for lack of anything more probable. The more I looked at it, the more it resembled a man hugged tight to the tree trunk." The redheaded sergeant cleared his throat.

Jones and the redheaded sergeant argued a minute or so about whether Jones had spotted a man or just another tree knot. The argument stopped when Jones saw the tree knot move and got himself ready for a possible kill. He recalled later that "a slight breeze drifted across the field from left to right, stirring with its breath a few pale spears of grass. I clicked in with a degree of windage and clicked one up on elevation. The workings were smooth. I kept them that way. The good sun provided me a sharp picture through the scope, although the foliage concealed most of what I at first mistook to be a 'knot.'"

Jones drew a deep breath, thought about the two Americans this sniper in the branches above him just shot, and tickled the rifle trigger ever so slowly. "I saw the tree shaking violently. The 'knot' seemed to be throbbing and pulsating. I quickly bolted in another round and put my cross hairs back on target. Sometimes you had to hit a squirrel [back in Tennessee] two or three times when it was high in the reaches of some sycamore or cottonwood and all you could get the first time was a piece of him." Jones squeezed off another round and watched as "the German turned loose just like a squirrel does and bounced off the limbs down through the tree until his body hit the ground."

A few minutes later, as Jones and his company walked past the corpse, he could see that the sniper was "just a kid" with sandy hair. The first bullet had caught him in the ribs and the second shot opened the German's chest. This was the only confirmed kill Jones had in the entire war. And when his 1903 Springfield with the scope was destroyed by an enemy mortar round, a few hours later, he became just another guy in the infantry.

Sometimes, infantry regulars became snipers simply by finding and using a German sniper rifle.

Texan Charles "Boots" Askins served in the US Border Patrol before the Japanese bombed Pearl Harbor. Since he was then too old to serve in an infantry unit at the decrepit age of thirty-two, Boots settled for a commission as a combat salvage unit officer but managed to find time on the front line working as a sniper.

Early 1945 found Askins and his salvage unit on the River Rur in Duren, fifty-two miles southwest of Cologne, looking at the German army across the water, with some time on his hands and an M-1 rifle on his shoulder. His driver, a Greek-American named Papalexiou, joined him in the overwatch set up in a ruined house one morning. Askins recalled later that "there were likely targets during the morning but the sun was all wrong." Since the sun was right in his eyes, he waited. After a few hours, the sun was finally behind him. The Big Greek helped him move a large comfortable divan beneath a shattered window. Askins rested his rifle on the back of the couch pointing out the window and waited. "Very directly a Wehrmachter [slang for a German soldier] sauntered down to a fringe of bushes within thirty feet of the river, hung his rifle on a nearby branch, slipped out of his greatcoat, hung it on another bush, and pulled down his pants. That didn't surprise me in the least." Askins recalled that he had been watching this very man for three days or so. "I could set my watch by his bowels." Askins remembered that this particular German seemed to be daring the Americans to disturb his latrine time. "He was behind the screen of bushes but I could see the outline of his hunkered body very plainly. I held for his big middle and meticulously squeezed off the shot. On the recoil of the M1 . . . I promptly snapped in another round. The Big Greek, who was watching through the binoculars, turned to me grinning. 'Both shots hit him. I saw the body jerk.'"

Concerned that they might be reprimanded rather than rewarded by the regular infantry officers all around them, they quickly left their hide but returned to the area when time permitted three days later. This time they picked a hide just across the river from buildings that the Allied bombardment had missed, where German soldiers might be temporarily living. Askins thought that "one appeared to be a school or possibly it was a monastery, for there were a whole series of windows which faced towards the river and all of which, of course, were shattered."

After staring at the building for a while, Askins thought that he saw something unusual in a corner window on the 3rd floor in a deep shadow. "It finally occurred to me that this was a big spotting scope. It had the right size for about a 40X, set on a heavy tripod, and as I kept my eyes glued to the scope, I was delighted to see that sitting comfortably behind the eyepiece was a Kraut soldier." Askins thought that this was an observer for the artillery or a mortar team. "As the sun marched in its usual fashion, the light into the room grew stronger. At the elbow of the observer was a field telephone and there was a field table, and watching keenly, I saw that the man did not give too much attention to his glass [spotting scope]. It was obvious he had been there for days, maybe even weeks, and was pretty bored with the job."

Askins considered this German to be a made-to-order target but there was one problem. The target was about four hundred meters (about 436 yards) away. Even so, Askins decided to take a shot at about 4:00 p.m. that afternoon when the six-foot broad-shouldered trooper stood up next to his observation telescope, offering a target centered within a window frame. Taking him down brought four more Germans into the room, all of which Askins and the Big Greek took out before quitting for the day.

— ⌒ —

Daniel Webster Cass Jr. spent April Fool's Day 1945 just off the beach at Okinawa. It was also Easter Sunday. Many of the veterans on board the transport waiting to do the landing took turns talking about their childhood Easter experiences while they all waited to wade through the water onto the sand. Or so they hoped. Cass and the other new guys didn't sleep much the night before. Instead they passed the time cleaning rifles, bayonets, and ammunition or playing poker on a blanket. On the bunks around him, Cass could see Bibles, letters from sweethearts, and a few paperback books.

The veterans talked incessantly of landings past and the terrain they would be facing at sunrise. "Did you see the way the hills come right down to the water?" asked one such veteran. The only thing Cass could do when he heard that talk was oil down his 1903 Springfield, clean it again with a cloth, and hope for the best tomorrow. After that was finished, Cass looked through the scope for the hundredth time to make sure that his view of tomorrow's targets would be perfectly clear. His partner Chester Carter had been with him since training days at the Camp Pendleton sniper school that was once a cattle ranch. Carter was eighteen, a year younger than Cass, who looked back fondly on what they had been through together so far, training both in California and the Russell Islands in the Central Province of the Solomons. They had mastered maps, scouting, and compass reading. More importantly, they spent hour after hour on night exercises. Cass was lost in thought about those times when a hollow-eyed, sunken-cheeked veteran sauntered up next to his bunk.

"You guys ever done any of this sniping before?" the grunt asked. When Cass told him this was his first mission, all the man could do was shake his head and wish them luck.

When the sun rose that Easter, they watched a bombardment of the Japanese positions so massive that Cass wondered out loud how anybody could have lived through it. "That's what we thought at Tarawa," somebody behind him whispered, just before they heard that first order putting others into combat.

"Carter and I flattened ourselves against the bulkhead out of the way, secretly relieved that we weren't among the first waves. Marines clambered down the rope nets like swarms of gray green ants." Cass remembered the clang of weapons, everyone sweating beneath the machine guns and mortars they were carrying, and the sadness of stepping on the fingers and helmets of the men below them. Weapons clanged. Men sweated beneath the burden of machine guns and mortars.

Cass and Carter watched the others go ashore and then followed with the headquarters group, after most of the main action was over, and spent the next thirty days or so watching the American armada bomb southern Okinawa. Finally, Cass, Carter, and the rest of the First Marines were ordered south to a mountain range where an infantry division was fighting Japanese soldiers from cave to cave. On the way in, they passed hundreds of bloody, limping, ragged army GIs walking through Japanese corpses bunched together like dead cows, on their way to a new daily routine.

"Artillery coughed day and night. It seemed the [Japanese] always counterattacked around midnight. The fighting raged out ahead of headquarters. Snipers got the word to go forward whenever pockets of Japanese snipers or machine gun nests pinned down our guys." Cass remembered darting, crawling, and fighting his way from downed trees to splintered stumps to shell craters, "through mud that was like a freshly plowed field after a downpour, working your way to the high ground if you could, so you could shoot down into the enemy positions."

Cass later recalled one particular mission in the Wanu Gorge Valley where Japanese machine guns pinned down an entire Marine Company on the floor of a valley which Cass and Carter could see from a ridge above. "It was like having the front row seat to a movie. The voices of the Marines on the floor of the valley sounded thin and reedy as they were whipped to shreds by the rapid Clack! Clack! Clack! of the Japanese machine guns." He watched marines run as quickly as they could through a field of shell craters. "They sprawled motionless behind whatever cover they could find. A few of them lay in the open. They were dead. Nips high on the ridge opposite from us sprayed them with a deadly hail of lead."

Cass and Carter were at least 1,200 yards away from the machine gun nests. Cass used his rifle scope to look for the Japanese across the valley. Carter finally found them but only after they watched yet another American take a head shot and tumble to the ground down in the valley. Carter was frantic now.

"See that cave, five o'clock from that telephone pole?" Cass followed Carter's finger pointing to a spot just below a coral ledge honeycombed with shallow caves. Cass remembered that "the nest was well camouflaged and dug in, but I detected a thin screen of smoke coming from what appeared to be a toppled underbrush. The smoke was a little bluer than that made by shellfire, and it was darker than the shredded remnants of fog." Cass didn't detect any wind but "the gun smoke clung to the air above the boulders and felled trees, Pinpoint muzzle flame flickered from the shadows. Two, maybe three guns were rattling from that location."

Carter, now serving as a spotter for Cass, was anything but confident, since the targets were some twelve football fields away. No doubt he was also worried about the variables that had to be dealt with in making such long shots. The wind, heat, and today a significant fog cover all had to be taken into account as Cass looked at the muzzle flames coming from two or maybe even three Japanese weapons. Cass started the "zeroing in" process by firing at a telephone just above the Japanese machine gunners to assure himself that he had the proper range. After the first shot, Cass could see that the marines in the valley below him were out of time. He had to act right now. He turned the scope elevation knob and dropped cross hairs onto the Japanese machine gun nest. "The Nips had to expose themselves at least a little in order to pivot their gun barrels toward the valley floor. I heard Carter murmur something . . . as I narrowed my concentration against [sic] a tiny patch of grayish uniform exposed above a tree trunk. I tried to remember everything I had learned at Camp Pendleton about long-distance shooting." That day, everything seemed to depend on what Cass had learned about sniping. "Smoke curled from behind the logs as the Nambu [Japanese machine gun] commenced to chatter its short repetitive phrases. *Deep breath. Let half out. Hold. Cross-hair, cross-hair, squeeze!*"

Cass remembered in detail what happened next. "With the spotter scope, you could actually pick up the streak of the bullet going through the air. Carter grunted 'All *right*' when my first round plunged into the enemy barricade." Later he remembered the sense of accomplishment this brought. "I worked the bolt with a feeling of elation. My hands and breathing were surprisingly steady. I fired and worked the bolt, fired and worked the bolt, pouring accurate fire into the Japanese defenses, cross-hairing handkerchief sized targets momentarily exposed more than half a mile away. Even through his spotting scope, Carter couldn't tell when I scored because the targets were so fleeting they disappeared whether I made a hit or not, but he was all grins."

Now both Carter and Cass welcomed the silence that replaced the Japanese machine gun fire chapter. Even better, Carter yelled, "They're running!" Cass could see for himself how this was going to turn out. "Several minute figures scurried out from the barricades like rats smoked out of a barn. I released a parting shot as they vanished over the ridge top. That was when I took a deep, wavering breath. I remembered what the captain said before we left the ship: 'We expect you to do your job.'

"I had done my job, hadn't I?"

CHAPTER EIGHT

A Swift and Silent Killer

SIMO HAYHA, THE MOST ACCOMPLISHED SNIPER IN WORLD HISTORY, died at age ninety-six, seven months after the 9/11 attacks, having killed some 542 Russians during the little-known 1939–1940 Winter War between the Soviet Union and Finland. Known as the "White Killer," "White Death," or, more commonly, the "White Sniper" for his ability to blend into the background of the snow through which he traveled, his luck at last ran out on March 6, 1940, just a few days before the war ended. The massive head wound he received that day at the hands of the Russians dogged him the rest of his long life.

We now know that the Soviet Union initiated the aggression against Finland on November 26, 1939, by lobbing several artillery shells near the Russian village of Mainila near the Finnish border and blaming Finland. When Finland refused to apologize, the Russians moved several divisions onto the Russian-Finnish border and attacked in full force with some twenty-three divisions composed of 450,000 troops the very next day. Three days later, the Russians created a puppet government at Terijoki, Finland.

Simo was thirty-four when the war with Russia began. Born in the Grand Duchy of Finland near the Russian border, slight, straight-backed Simo grew up as the second youngest of eight children in a devout, observant Lutheran household. Deciding at age twenty that he no longer wanted to farm, he joined a Finnish militia called the White

Guard and quickly earned a reputation for good marksmanship and earned a bunker locker full of trophies to prove it.

When the Winter War began, Simo was taking an anti-tank course but on the last day of November he learned about the heavy Russian bombardments that meant he would soon be going into combat. He left Suvilahti, Finland, to meet his comrades in the Viipuri Civil Guard now bound for a place called Pyhajoki. And there, they began assembling what they needed to fight this war, or so they thought. Simo later recalled that "we assembled our barbed wire, fortified our trenches and finished digging our fox holes. The first Soviet attack against us came during the darkness. After a few days of heavy fighting, we were given orders to withdraw all the way to Suvilahti." Soon Simo and the others engaged the Russians again, just before an engagement he never forgot. "I was given a mission to destroy the telephone line. I did that and cut the wires, taking my time, although the Russians were shooting at me with a machine gun from a position about 200 meters [2018 yards] away. I just couldn't think yet that I would be in any real danger as our losses in Pyhajoki had been very low despite the heavy fighting and bombardment."

All too soon Simo fought in some of the first battles of the war. Eventually, his unit fell back with much of the Finnish army to the River Kollaa. There, heroic stands by the outnumbered army soon had all of Finland believing that no matter what, the Kollaa Front would hold. But now, in the early days of the Winter War, Simo's company commander Lieutenant Juutilainen quickly realized that Simo should work alone or in small groups as a sniper, as his principal biographer Tapio A. M. Saarelainen recounted in his biography *The White Sniper: The Deadliest Sniper in History*. Simo's first target was a Russian sniper who had killed three platoon leaders and a courier. This was the first time Simo wore the gear that eventually earned him the moniker: the White Sniper.

He picked a good firing spot, pulled on layer after layer of white clothing topped by snow-camouflaged fatigues, giving himself the appearance of a snowman. And then he waited. Daylight was slowly coming to an end. Evening drew closer. After several hours of waiting,

Simo noticed a flicker on the horizon—the last rays of sunlight reflecting directly off the Russian sniper's scope. In addition, the Russian rose rather carelessly, most likely believing that with the dusk approaching his day's work was done. Simo carefully aimed, squeezed the trigger, and hit him on the cheek. Although Simo instinctively reloaded his rifle, there was no need for a second shot. The Russian was dead.

Soon, Simo had another sniping opportunity. This time he cleaned up again for his company commander Lieutenant Juttilainen, who tried to kill a Russian sniper himself. "It happened once that my CO, Lieutenant Juttilainen, 'the Horror of Morocco' as he was known from his previous service in the [French] Foreign Legion, tired to kill an enemy sniper with a scoped rifle," Simo remembered. "This Russian had taken up a position about 400 meters from us and was constantly shooting towards our lines. After a while, the lieutenant sent for me and showed me approximately where he thought the enemy sniper's position to be. One of our second lieutenants was with us, acting as a spotter when our duel began." Simo didn't see him at first but eventually "spotted him behind a little hump of snow near that rock. I took a careful aim with my trusty M/28–30 and the very first shot hit the intended target."

Soon after the war began, Simo was called away from his normal duties to deal with a Russian spotting periscope being used to bring heavy artillery in on his battalion. His commanding officer sent him to destroy it. Simo recalled, "There was another forward observer who was preparing to fire for effect. I only got two or three shots at the forward observer's periscope before the Russians started to shoot at us with heavy artillery fire. Shrapnel, tree branches and ash were flying all over the place, but miraculously, we survived." The mission had to be aborted before the enemy spotting periscope was destroyed.

Later that day, Simo returned to take the Russian periscope out, drawing even more heavy artillery fire into the 5th company bunkers. Later, he took out the second Russian spotting periscope as well.

A corporal Malmi served as Simo's spotter for much of his sniper work. "In early February [1940], Corporal Malmi and I spotted a new area of enemy accommodation [*sic*] bunkers," Simo recalled later. "The two of us set out to an observations post to learn what was going on there. We moved silently through the forest and got within 150 meters of the enemy bunkers, which were located between the front lines. We spent the whole day in our position and killed 19 Russians. They never learned where we were and dared not send a patrol out under that circumstance."

After this, the Russians in Simo's area covered their bunkers and connecting trenches with walls of snow to avoid detection. During the first few weeks of the ninety-eight days in which Simo kill 542 Russians, he trekked to his sniper hide early in the morning and did not return until late evening, spending many of his nights in Lieutenant Juutilainen's spacious tent.

On Thursday, December 21, 1939, Simo scored twenty-five official, confirmed kills of Russian soldiers, beating his prior day record by two, having already killed more than one hundred other Russian soldiers by that day. Christmas 1939 became a special memory for Simo, who had added fifty-one additional confirmed kills to his death before Yuletide. His sniper hides were positioned to give him a side angle view of the Russians he targeted. When his numbers approached two hundred confirmed kills, gifts including several fine pocket watches poured in from his hometown and the region around it. Soon a package from his commanding general containing handmade gloves no doubt knitted by the general's wife.

Outnumbered and outequipped though they were, the legendary Finnish "forest warriors" along the Kollaa Front kept the Russians in check. This was no easy feat, since two-3rds of the entire Finnish army was confined to a relatively small space with very little room to maneuver against the enemy. The one distinct advantage they possessed was a familiarity with the terrain. This gave Finnish headquarters confidence in planning tactical and operational maneuvers that often outweighed Russian numerical strength in localized battles.

Years later, the Finnish chaplain Rantamaa recalled how he had proposed awarding a custom-built precision Sako rifle to Simo with a citation honoring his sniper record as it stood in mid-February 1940.

"This honorary rifle from Sweden is granted to NCO Simo Hayha in recognition of his great accomplishments as a shooter and combatant. His deeds, 219 enemies shot with a rifle and the same number with a machine gun shows what a determined Finnish man who fears nothing can do, has sharp eyes and whose hands do not shake."

The same citation suggested that Simo consider the rifle equal to a medal to be passed down "as a reminder for the yet unborn generations of the great deeds done by Simo Hayha in the great war when the men of Finland bravely and with success fought for the freedom of their country, the future of their people and for the greater ideals of mankind." In this spirit, Simo never used the Sako rifle, which now resides in a brigade museum. Immediately after the war ceremony he returned to the Kolla battlefront, shouldering his standard Finnish M/28-30 rifle for the most critical phase of the Winter War.

Simo now led his own squad in desperate conventional battles against overwhelming numbers of Russians, killing another forty enemies, according to his own calculations, in the forests of Ulisuma. On Wednesday, March 6, 1940, Simo's luck in battle ran out. Just as some Russians began breaking through the Finnish lines, an explosive bullet struck Simo in the jaw. When he awoke from a coma one week later, the Winter War was over.

There are several descriptions of how exactly the Russians attacked Simo and how he survived. The most widely accepted told by Pastor Rantamaa explains that "his remarkable battle career ended at 14:00 hours (2:00 p.m.) on March 6 in the heavy battles of Ulismainen after making a new personal record which was 40 Russians killed." The clergymen recorded that despite this "there were hordes of Russians coming from all directions and it was simply impossible to fight them all off with a bolt-action rifle." Finally, one of the Russians got close enough to shoot Simo through the upper jaw with an explosive bullet.

This left Simo with his entire upper left jaw blown away. The same happened to the lower left jaw which the bullet tore into two pieces. It seemed to be the end of the story or so thought his comrades as they settled him on his back in the Lapp sledge for evacuation. It seemed even more like an instant death as Simo had by instinct turned on his stomach face down to the ground as if he wanted to die in the position where he had remarkably ended the lives of so many enemies before. Now it was the end of his life, thought his comrades as they looked with sad eyes as he was evacuated—to the grave as they thought. In man-pulled Lapp sledge (sled) they took him away.

Finland awarded the Kollaa Cross to Simo that June. Due to the severity of his wounds, Simo could not speak or eat solid food for three months and nearly died. During the course of some twenty-six operations, Danish Dr.s reconstructed his jaw and released him in May 1941. Simo farmed with his brother for two decades, established his own farm in the 1960s, and died as the most decorated and honored warrior in modern Finland on April 1, 2002.

In the years since his death, some observers have questioned the number of sniper kills credited to Simo. Nevertheless, official Finnish Army records, supplemented by the contemporaneous diary of the military chaplain Antti Rantamaa documented 138 Simo Hayha sniper kills by December 22, 1939, another 61 kills by January 26, 1940, 20 more by February 17, 1940, and yet another 40 by March 6, the day he was wounded. Thus official records attribute 259 sniper kills to Simo Hayha. Chaplain Rantamaa attributed an equal number of machine gun kills to Hayha, strongly suggesting an estimate of some sort. These things said, no one has ever questioned the bravery or skill of Simo Hayha, the White Sniper.

CHAPTER NINE

A Sniper and a Historian

Dark-headed Lyudmila Pavlichenko killed some 309 Germans and German allies if the official record is to be believed. Martin Pegler, one of the most distinguished historians specializing in the study of firearms in general and snipers in particular, opines that the exact Lyudmila total is really unknown, but five hundred kills would not be improbable. In an environment where Soviet snipers often served in combat no more than two weeks, Lyudmila lived to tell the tale of those five hundred kills and toured the United States, Canada, and the United Kingdom to whip up support for the Allied war effort. Eventually, Lyudmila Pavlichenko began writing the unfinished memoir *Lady Death: The Memoirs of Stalin's Sniper*, which served as the primary source for this chapter.

Hundreds of women in the Soviet Union became army snipers during World War II, Lyudmila being only the most successful and well known. She earned award upon award, spent face time with the notorious dictator Joseph Stalin, and eventually became a naval historian. Lyudmila grew up the daughter of a Russian Communist bureaucrat named Belova and his wife, a language teacher. He worked in Boguslav in the Kiev Region but eventually transferred to Bila Tserkva, then the capital of the Ukraine, when Lyudmila was fourteen. From an early age, Lyudmila absorbed military history in every spare moment.

Otherwise, her early life paralleled that of other young women in Kiev, playing Cossacks and bandits rather than cops and robbers, splashing around in the River Ros, and stealing apples from a local orchard. She just turned fifteen when she met a man named Pavlichenko, married him, and gave birth to a son named Rostislav. Soon Pavlichenko simply disappeared and at the prompting of her father, Lyudmila began working in an Arsenal factory built 148 years earlier at the direction of Catherine the Great. During Lyudmila's time there, the Arsenal produced rifles, bayonets, and other armaments, as well as ploughs, locks, and horse carts. Her sixteenth birthday brought acceptance into the Young Communists League and a new hobby: shooting. The firing range was just outside the Arsenal and stocked with nearly new TOZ-8 rifles. The TOZ was a small-bore, single-shot rifle that Lyudmila used to become a sharpshooter. Lyudmila came to think of firearms as "the most perfect creation of human mind and hand. Their construction always made use of the latest innovations." she recalled. "The technological solutions necessary for their manufacture were quickly refined and put into a production process that output thousands and millions of items. In the case of the most successful models, those worthy of world recognition engineering genius finds its fulfillment in an ideal and consummate external shape." Lyudmila saw these weapons as akin to works of art. "They are pleasant to pick up and convenient to use. They earned the love of the people who took them into wars of unbelievable ferocity. Some of them (the Mosin Three Line Rifle, the Shpagin submachine gun, the Degtyarev light machine gun and the Tula-Tokarev pistol) have even become unique symbols of their era."

Her marksmanship became both a passion and a diversion, but one at which she excelled. She earned honorary certificates in shooting competitions but recalled later that "I was unable to explain what drew me to the shooting range, what was attractive about an object equipped with a metal barrel, a wooden butt, a breech, a trigger and sights, and why it was so interesting to control the flight of a bullet toward its target."

The year 1935 found sixteen-year-old Lyudmila working as a draftsman at the Arsenal while also studying history in the evenings at Kiev State University, just a year before war began in Spain. Two years later, she accepted an invitation to attend a new sniper school established in Kiev. "Sessions were held twice a week: on Wednesdays from six to eight in the evening and on Saturdays from three in the afternoon until six in the evening. The students wore dark blue tunics at all times. All this was reminiscent of army rules, but we did not complain; on the contrary we were infused with a serious attitude and an awareness of our responsibility given the prospect of the lessons ahead."

She excelled at examinations that lasted as long as sixteen hours. Lyudmila and other students who excelled went on to shooting competitions.

After many of the initial students had been eliminated, the course became more difficult and complex. Lyudmila later remembered that "slowly but relentlessly Potapov [the instructor] taught us to observe the surrounding world closely, to examine keenly the details of life's rapid pace, as if through telescope sights, to gain a concept of the whole picture from minor details. With this approach, there was always something losing its significance, receding into or merging into the background. Or something would become particularly important, as if magnified by a lens."

Then the students were introduced to the art and science of "ballistics: in particular we were given an understanding of distance estimation, were taught how to calculate the range quickly according to angles, using a special formula; how far the rapidly rotating bullet would drift laterally through its travel from the muzzle to the target."

That spring they began traveling through the countryside where Potapov taught them the methods of camouflage and "the feeling for the target" that a sniper develops through training. Lyudmila graduated from sniper school just before Germany attacked Poland and World War II began. Her father, who had sensitive confidential information as a consequence of his government position, soon began to intimate to his family that tough times were ahead. Even so, life went on much as it had. Lyudmila graduated from sniper school, resumed her night classes at the university, and became the head of acquisitions at the state history library, now helping support her family.

Even better, she soon began a four-month assignment at the Odessa Library, three hundred miles south of Kiev, as a senior research assistant, all of which would enable her to finish a dissertation. Now, all that stood between Lyudmila and her college diploma was World War II.

June 22, 1941, started as an ordinary Sunday or so it seemed to Lyudmila, now living in Odessa under a clear blue sky next to the smooth blue surface of the Black Sea, stretching out to an endless horizon. That idyllic day turned somber when "Comrade Molotov" announced on radio that their German allies had attacked the Soviet Union at 4:00 a.m. that morning.

Lyudmila enjoyed a performance of *La Traviata* that night, knowing that the next day she would report to the Odessa military commissariat for service. Two days later, she sat on a train full of recruits traveling west toward her new assignment with the 25th Chapayev Rifle Division, 54th Stepan Razin Rifle Regiment, digging trenches in Bessarabia, present-day Moldava. Her only weapon was a hand grenade.

During July, the 25th Division moved four different times, traveling by truck and two-horse carts across the steppes, while cannons volleyed in the distance. They drove through hundreds of small carts bearing families and everything they now possessed, traveling as fast as they could away from the war that could be heard in the near distance. Twin-engined German reconnaissance planes often flew above them on Lyudmila's journey. All too soon they watched German Stuka dive bombers swoop down on the civilians as the 54th hid in nearby forests for want of artillery, rifles, and even ammunition.

Trench warfare on the Novo-Pavlosk line against Romanians in mid-July brought Lyudmila a standard Mosin model 1891/1930 ("Three Line") rifle from another soldier so severely wounded he couldn't fight anymore. She remembered that incident all too well. "Drenched in blood, he handed his Three Line to me. After some preliminary artillery fire, the Romanians prepared to attack and together with the other soldiers of our 1st Platoon, I placed my rifle on the parapet of the shallow trench, set the back sight on mark

3 (that is, for a distance of 300 meters) and pulled back the bolt."
She remembered that first action in exacting detail. "Thrusting the
bolt forward ensure that there was a cartridge in the chamber and a
light bullet . . . awaiting its release. At the command of Junior
Lieutenant Kovtun we opened fire, The Company light machine
guns also went into action."

This minor engagement turned on making a successful counterattack. Lyudmila and the others climbed out of their trenches and drove
the Fascists far behind that line where the Fascists started. Then, the
"54th Regiment went about gathering up the weapons of the enemy
dead." The trophies included 7.9mm-caliber vz.24 Czech Mauser
rifles. "Our cartridges did not fit them, so we were also required to take
the cartridge bags from the bodies. Of course this only partially solved
our soldiers' weapon problems."

Lieutenant Kovtun had watched Lyudmila perform in battle and
promised her that she soon would become a sniper. Eventually she did
just that, but now she joined the rest of the 54th Regiment in a retreat
made acceptable only by the arrival of the light machine guns, rifles,
and ammunitions that the regiment desperately needed. Lyudmila
received a new Mosin sniper rifle still caked with factory grease.

The German and Romanian enemies outnumbered the Russians
five to one, but the Russians fought on. Friday, August 8, 1941,
found Lyudmila and her comrades on the outskirts of Odessa at
one of the many places in that part of the world called Belyayevka;
this Belyayevka was about forty kilometers from Odessa near a lake
called Byeloye. Clay cottages with reed roofs surrounded a church, a
school, and a few houses made of stone. Soon, the commander called
Lyudmila to the command post on the front line for an assignment.
Once again Lyudmila later remembered this in exacting detail. "Visible
there among the overgrown trees was a large house with a porch which
had a ridged roof, well illuminated by the setting sun. Two men came
out onto the porch in officers' uniforms and helmets reminiscent of
rustic pudding basins. The kingdom of Romania had bought up these
steel [helmets] for its army from their Dutch suppliers before the
war." Now her commander gave Lyudmila an offer she couldn't refuse.

"Looks like that's the staff headquarters. Can you reach it?" asked the battalion commander. "I'll try, Comrade Captain." She replied. "Go on then," said the commander as he stepped away giving her room to work.

Years later, Lyudmila described her first kills on August 8. "The rifle was over my shoulder and from my belt hung three leather pouches containing cartridges sorted by type . . . I took the rifle in my hands and looked through the eyepiece of the telescope sight. The horizontal line covered the figure of the officer descending the steps, approximately down to his waist." Next, she mentally went through a mathematical equation "from the course in practical ballistics which we had done at the school and the solution was: distance to the target, 400 meters." Next, she loaded the rifle and looked for a location from which to shoot.

"The captain and I were in the middle of a peasant hut which had been destroyed by a direct hit from a shell. The roof was smashed in, and stones and charred splinters of beams were spread around everywhere. It did not appear possible to fire from a lying position." She decided to shoot from behind a wall on one knee, resting on the heel of her right boot. She decided to "lean on my left bent knee with my left elbow and to let the strap under the left elbow carry the weight of the rifle. Not for nothing did Potapov often remind us of the sniper saying: 'It's the barrel that fires, but the gunstock that hits!' A lot depends on the position which the marksman adopts when holding the rifle."

Lyudmila recalled, "I hit the first target with the 3rd shot and the second one on my fourth attempt, having loaded the rifle with one of the scarce cartridges containing the 'D'-type heavy bullets." She didn't hesitate nor was she nervous. "What hesitation can there be after three weeks of desperate retreat under enemy bombs and shells?" Despite this, something distracted her. "They say this sometimes happens when a sniper first makes the transition from shooting practice at cardboard targets to firing at live [enemies]."

"Lucy," said the battalion commander sympathetically, not remembering her real name, looking through the binoculars at the enemy officers lying motionless by the porch. "You need to conserve cartridges. Seven on two Nazis, that's a lot."

She apologized, promised she would do better, and did just that. The Russians replenished their armaments with weapons and the ammunition picked up from the Romanians and the Germans that they killed. Still, as Lucy recalled later, acquiring abundant arms at the expense of their enemies didn't mean that all trouble was behind the 25th Chapayev Rifle Division.

"However boldly we Chapayevs fought, the harsh conditions of the battle for Odessa sometimes got the better of us. The enemy enjoyed superiority in artillery and, most important, had huge military supplies for ordnance and mortars which the city [Odessa] lacked." She remembered with some bitterness that "our gunners could only respond with one salvo to every three fired by the Germans and the Romanians." On the morning of August 19, she recalled, "Our company was once smothered by a wave of fire. A mortar shell hit the trench parapet, not right in front of me, but about 2 meters to the left. The shock wave smashed my beloved rifle to smithereens, threw me backwards into the bottom of the trench and covered me with earth." She awoke in a hospital bed in Odessa, lucky to be alive.

When released from the hospital at the end of August, Lyudmila briefly stopped in Odessa on her way back to the front where she learned that she had been promoted to corporal. Sadly, Lieutenant Kovtun and another thirty soldiers had died in the ten days she had been gone. The Odessa defense district now expected Lyudmila and the other snipers to give the German and Romanian enemies no peace. The snipers were expected to identify and occupy the most advantageous positions for observing, firing on the enemy, and depriving him of the opportunity to move freely. These orders didn't surprise Lyudmila or the other snipers, but the challenges carrying them out were significant. The terrain consisted of largely flat steppes with a few small hills here and there, no trees, and few ideal sniper hides. After extensive discussions, Lyudmila and the other snipers decided to operate in the no-man's-land between the lines as close to the enemies as possible. In her first mission after returning from hospital, Lyudmila and two other soldiers equipped themselves with a light machine gun, gas mask bags filled with cartridges, and as many grenades as could be attached to their belts.

The trio picked a sniper hide in a dense thicket of tall shrubs roughly in the shape of a diamond about 150 meters (165 yards) long and 16 meters wide about 600 meters from their fox hole on the Russian front lines. Years later, she described their first night sniping here. "On exiting the dugout after midnight, we took an hour to cover the distance to the hideout. The moon in the cloudless sky illuminated the surroundings, and all the pathways, uneven patches and shell holes showed up clearly. The quiet, warm gentle Black Sea night embraced the countryside around us." According to Lyudmila's recollections, neither side did much shooting at first. "All around, it was so nice, so peaceful! Only the likelihood of a meeting with the enemy right in the shrub thicket spoiled our mood." Lyudmila and the others had to keep their weapons ready at all times. "There turned out to be no Romanians in the thicket. Why they had not occupied it and at least stationed an observation post there we could not understand." She attributed this to "Gypsy fecklessness," whatever that might be. "The punctual and calculating Germans had tried and tried to teach their [Romanian] allies about modern warfare, but they had not succeeded" or so she said.

Lyudmila and her partners spent the rest of the night digging and reinforcing their sniping positions with stones and turf, working out the distances to their prospective targets, and helping their machine gunner set up his position. Their next objective was scouting their targets, in detail. "It grew light. At five o'clock in the morning there was some movement in the enemy lines. The soldiers walked around fully upright, talked loudly and called out to one another. Breakfast arrived at six that morning, and then things became livelier. Officers appeared and gave loud orders. At some distance away stood what was probably a medical station; the gleaming white smocks of the medics were clearly discernible to us."

She relished remembering that enemy targets were visible everywhere. "We divided our forces: the left flank would be mine . . . The machine-gunner kept the centre under observation. We waited till ten o'clock in the morning, studying how the enemy behaved when they were some distance from the front line, and then we opened fire." She remembered the palpable fear they created in the Romanians. "For several minutes they could not work out where the shots were coming from and rushed around, intensifying the panic with their wild wailing. But we had measured the range and our sights were adjusted. Almost every bullet found its target. In approximately twenty minutes Kolokoltsev [another sniper] and I took seventeen shots each. The result: sixteen kills to me and Pyotr had twelve. The machine-gunner, who was supposed to cover us in the event of direct enemy attack on our hideout, did not fire because there was no need."

Despite this, the Romanians managed to open fire on Lyudmila and the other Russians in the thicket. "However, they could not see us and therefore their shooting was off the mark. We had to get away. We made it back to our own lines, wrote our report for our regimental commander and received an official message of gratitude for our bold action."

The next night Lyudmila's trio returned to the same hideout and discovered that some Romanian soldiers had visited the place and left six bottles of sweet wine, not expecting the Russians to return for more sniping. The trio started sniping again at noon. "It was a repeat of the previous day's scene: I had ten kills, including two officers, while Pyotr Kolokoltsev got eight." Yet there was something different this time. "The Romanians quickly recovered their composure and began to fire back at the thicket with two machine guns. The rounds came closer and closer to our trenches. We ceased fire, withdrew, moved inconspicuously to one side and approached the machine-gunners from the flank." Recalling that day in 1974, Lyudmila wrote, "From a distance of 100 meters we took five shots with our sniper rifles and wiped out the squad. Pyotr liked the enemy machine guns; they were quite new and all the components shone. In brief, we took one machine gun away with us and buried the breechblock of the other." Later, Russian scouts found the breechblock and the machine gun and kept both as trophies. "There were ample boxes of cartridges lying around, and the

Austrian machine guns went on to serve the Red Army," she recalled, but now it was time to move. "It would have been irrational to use this spot as a sniper hideout for a 3rd time. Therefore we found another one, a white house which was half destroyed and had been abandoned by its residents."

Early in September 1941, Lyudmila and the rest of her 54th Regiment were confronted by something highly unusual: "The sounds of stirring music reached our ears. We saw that the [Romanian] infantry in their pudding-basin helmets were not spreading out across the steppe, but on the contrary, sticking together in close, dense columns, standing shoulder to shoulder and marching as if on parade, raising their feet high to the rhythmic beat of the drums." She could see a banner over the soldier's heads in the second or 3rd column. "Keeping their distance and shouldering their unleashed sabers, the officers were striding along in the gaps between the columns. On the left flank was a priest in full garb." She recalled thirty-four years later that "his gold-embroidered gown, glinting in the rays of the bright autumn sun, looked strange against the monolithic military formation. Altogether the column was carrying three church banners."

"The priest, it subsequently turned out, was Ukrainian. It was not without some amazement that I viewed the attacking force through binoculars. They were approaching closer and closer." And then she noticed that all of the soldiers were drunk. "They were not maintaining their formation so strictly and their marching was not all that precise. But would it be possible to force sober men out onto an absolutely flat, easily targeted plain, even if they were convinced of their racial superiority over those they intended to exterminate?" Lyudmila guessed that they were overconfident because her side was vastly outnumbered. "Marching against our 1st Battalion, in which no more than 400 were left, to the sound of loud music from a military band, was an infantry regiment of peacetime proportions—2,000 bayonets."

Lyudmila waited patiently as they approached, planning how she would deal with a fence some six hundred meters away as thousands of men walked into her range of fire. "I had developed a favorite method of shooting by then," she recalled, "hitting the enemy between the eyes or in the temple. But as I looked at the infantry armada marching to the beat of the drum, I thought that this time a shot to the head alone would be an impermissible luxury. The main thing now was to fire and fire and fire, just to stop the psychological attack of drunken soldiers, who had no idea what they were doing, to prevent the Romanians from reaching our trenches. After all, with their five-fold numerical advantage, they would simply trample our valiant battalion into the ground and wipe out all my comrades."

Some three hundred Romanians died that day, nineteen of which Lyudmila claimed as her own by counting those who had been shot in the head, neck, or left side of their chest. Soon, her lieutenant promoted her to the rank of junior sergeant.

Late September found the 54th Regiment mounting an attack against Gildendorf, a town in southern Ukraine established by German settlers in the late nineteenth century. Lyudmila asked her lieutenant for permission to conduct sniping operations from the town cemetery.

And there she found a historically significant sniper hide. "Trees shaded the eternal resting place of Gildendorf's first burgomaster, the worthy Wilhelm Schmidt, who had died in 1899 according to the inscription on the marble monument. Planting my legs on the black slab, I began to clamber up the trunk of a mighty maple which leaned over the tomb."

That day, Lyudmila used a Mosin sniper rifle with PE sight, a belt with two ammunition pouches full of cartridges with "L" type light bullets and black-tipped B-30 armor-piercing bullets since she intended to kill the machine-gun crew and destroy their weapon. She also had a flask in a cloth cover and a Finnish-type army knife. "I did not take binoculars or a steel helmet, because my hearing had deteriorated following the shell shock and the helmet made it difficult for me to detect faint sounds," she explained in her memoir.

Minutes before sunrise, Lyudmila looked through her telescopic sight into the village, which consisted of one street straddled by monotonous one-story stone houses, a mill, a church, and a school; nearby in an orchard next to a ruined manor house, she discovered why the infantrymen in her regiment had sustained so many losses in the last few days: a German machine gun sporting telescopic sights.

Now Lyudmila formulated her plan of attack. "At seven o'clock in the morning the guard changed. However, the soldiers with rifles did not interest me. I was waiting for the machine-gunners. They appeared later, three Romanians in sandy gray jackets and kepis [caps] with their funny crowns stretched to form a double peak, front and back." She watched them set up their machine guns and then lie down for a snack from a pear tree orchard nearby.

While she took this in, Lyudmila developed yet another strategy. "I planned to take three shots, no more." She saved one of them for the back of the machine gun. "Inserting a cartridge with a light bullet into the barrel bore I closed the bolt and pressed my face close to the telescopic sight. The target, the head of a tall soldier sitting near the MG 34 tripod, was situated between the two black lines and only seconds remained before the shot was taken." Only then did she realize that something was going on in the orchard. "The machine-gunners leapt up, lined up, and froze at attention. A minute later some officers in peaked caps came up to them. One of them looked most interesting: a cigar in his mouth, a gold strip along the edge of his cap, a braided loop hanging from his right shoulder, a brown leather satchel at his side and a long whip in his hand. All in all, he had a haughty and authoritative air."

She calculated the distance to be about two hundred meters. "The wind had died down. The air temperature was approaching 25 degrees [77 degrees Fahrenheit]. I took as my target not the soldier but the man with the braided loop, held my breath, counted to myself . . . and smoothly pressed the trigger."

The Romanian soldiers heard her shot interrupt the morning quiet. "Still, it probably did not immediately cross their minds that a sniper was operating. The adjutant did not cry out as he keeled over. They [the Romanians] began to fuss around him, quite pointlessly as the bullet had hit him between the eyes. I managed to reload the rifle twice and both machine-gunners also ended up on the ground. The armor-piercing bullet from the fourth shot struck the breech of the MG 34 and put it out of commission."

Lyudmila injured her right hip jumping down from her sniping tree that morning and suffered in pain as the rest of her battalion assaulted and occupied Gildendorf. The adjutant that she shot reported directly to the Romanian dictator Major Gheorghiu Karaga. Important staff papers and a diary were found on his body, but Lyudmila accepted his cigar case as a trophy. Within days, Lyudmila received a special sniper rifle in recognition of her services. Eventually, she traveled to the United States, became a personal friend and correspondent with First Lady Eleanor Roosevelt, and died in 1974 at age fifty-eight, one of the most accomplished snipers in world history.

CHAPTER TEN

Shooting in the Cold:
The Korean Experience

THE END OF WORLD WAR II BROUGHT PEACE, IF ONLY BRIEFLY, EVEN as China, Russia, and the United States (the "Big Three") prepared for wars against each other. The emergence of 3rd World undeveloped nations provided the backdrop for proxy wars promoted or underwritten by the Big Three. 3rd World countries usually featured large populations governed by unstable leadership at best or, all too often, dictatorships.

Allied and Communist forces stood toe to toe in Berlin, while five thousand miles away an equally dangerous situation developed in Korea that had been divided at the 38th Parallel when World War II ended. The North Koreans rolled south in June 1950, maximizing their gains in many sectors through the use of Soviet-trained snipers equipped with Mosin-Nagant 1891/30 rifles fitted with telescopic sights. During the later stages of this three-year conflict, highly trained Chinese snipers joined them in the fight against South Koreans, Americans, and their allied forces.

Communist battle tactics were often copied by the Allies, as the war "degenerated at times into a protracted stand-off, with each side staging raids against the other's fortified trench lines, as well as undertaking intermittent mortar and artillery barrages. Operations were limited by harsh, mountainous terrain and winter temperatures which regularly reached well below zero degrees Fahrenheit."

The need to deploy American snipers became quite obvious to the commanding officer of the 3rd Battalion, 1st Marine Regiment one morning in 1951 as military historian Adrian Gilbert explained in *Stalk and Kill: The Sniper Experience*, the work largely relied upon in this chapter. "When the shell-scarred slopes became visible at first light, he placed his binoculars in the bunker opening and gazed out. Ping! A sniper bullet smashed the binoculars to the deck while blood welled up in the crease in his hand."

Fortunately the battalion commander was only slightly wounded "but he reflected it was a helluva situation when the CO could not even take a look at the ground he was defending without getting shot at. Right then and there he decided something had to be done about the enemy sniper. Now was the time to bring in the pin-wheel boys, the Marines who could keep every shot within the V ring at five hundred yards."

Combat engineer battalion veteran Bernie Resnick later told a New England newspaper correspondent that "constant sniper fire was the scariest part of the war. Snipers were in the hills; they were everywhere. And there were North Korean soldiers in civilian uniforms. On my first job of driving a grader, the sniper bullets were so close you could hear what sounded like the snapping of a whip at a circus. It was the sweetest sound in the world when you heard that because you knew the bullet had missed you."

Marine Sergeant Bill Krilling saw one close friend killed by a sniper only to see another friend killed by the same sniper while trying to retrieve Krilling's dead friend. "I decided there and then to become a sniper," Krilling recalled.

Francis H. Killeen had served in the marines during World War II, went to the USMC Scout Sniper School, and joined the 7th Marines in Korea. Eventually equipped with a M1903A4 Springfield rifle with an 8-power sight, he began sniper duty when the 7th was rushed to the front to engage a Chinese regiment.

Years later he recalled that "we got into a ditch alongside the road and I immediately figured our range would be 400 yards uphill. I looked through my 8-power scope and could spot an otherwise unseen line of riflemen firing down at us by seeing the 'fuzz' of their projectiles. Now was the time to act. Lieutenant Davis, our 60 mm mortar man, was right beside me. I told him where the enemy fire was coming from and in less than a minute he had three mortars in action and the fire lifted. We attacked and took the positions."

Until now he didn't really know whether to use his sniper weapon or standard issue M1 for such situations. "This was the first time I found my sniper gun to be more effective than my M1 rifle. Usually we were in close actions where the M1's rapid fire could be more important than the long range capability, but this time we were looking over a big valley at ridges 500 to 600 yards across the way. I chose a rock on the far ridge and got my lieutenant to spot my strikes with his binoculars. In that way, I made sure my rifle was still shooting where I aimed."

Late that afternoon, Killeen watched the enemy began moving into position for the evening. "I got off a couple of rounds, but without a spotter I could not tell if I was making hits. I got a BAR [Browning Automatic Rifle] man to register his rifle on the same rock I had used for zeroing. When he had his sights right we tried some team shooting."

Killeen even worked out a routine for the occasion. "When I located the enemy I fired tracer at him or them. Although tracer is lighter than the AP were using, the trajectory was close enough and the BAR man, who could not see the enemy with his iron sights, simply attempted to catch my tracer with his bullets. The idea was to hammer the enemy with a decent volume of fire in the hopes that if I missed, the BAR man would get him."

Soon other snipers working with BAR men started doing the same thing. "The technique was instantly popular, and I soon had a light machine-gun and two more BARs creating the biggest beaten zone I ever saw. My lieutenant, James Stemple, got more riflemen into the fray, and we had the enemy falling all along their wood line."

Killeen forgot all about the "hit and run" rules he was supposed to be following. He also forgot that there were other men around him who could shoot. "A bullet about one click low reminded me, and I cleared out just as a few more came into where I had just been."

Soon after this, Killeen had a close call while still fighting in the Su Dong Ni area. "The Chinese used mostly concussion grenades and one slipped in that knocked the wind out of me. I had a dozen pieces of shrapnel in my field jacket and leg. Most could have been removed with tweezers."

Even though the skirmish was quickly over, Killeen recalled, "I was lying there clutching my scoped rifle when someone pointed out a Chinese across the valley waving a red flag with other Red soldiers cheering him on. My last shot had been in close so I had to adjust the scope for 600 yards. I got into a hasty sling and fired at the flag waver. That shot may still be flying around North Korea because no one paid any attention," he quipped.

Killeen was ordered back to the aid station, but he had one last thing to take care of before he left. "The guy waving the red flag really annoyed me. Odd hand, with no sling, I even forgot to pull the scope back into position, I let a round go at the flag man. Down he went, right on his butt, and his Red Army cheering section hit the dirt." One of his superior officers saw this and called it a "damn fine shot." Killeen shrugged off the compliment or so he said.

Two years later in 1953, Army Corporal Chet Hamilton watched an assault near the legendary Pork Chop Hill. "The GIs who made it to the hill started up the slope. The grade was so steep they tugged at rocks and bushes to assist them. The more heavily burdened with machine guns and flamethrowers straggled, while skirmishers broke into little pockets to continue the assault."

Hamilton recalled feeling helpless until he noticed something. It was only about 400 yards across the valley from the Chinese lines. "My position put me on almost the same level with the Chinese defenders on the other hill. In order for the Chinese Communists to see our troops and fire at them down through their wire as the GIs charged up the hill, they had to lean up and out over their trenches, exposing wide patches of their quilted hides."

Hamilton later recalled that this was all he needed. "It had become clear morning in spite of the smoke and dust boiling above the Chinese hill. The four-power magnification of my scope made the [Chinese] leap right into my face." All he had to do now was work down the trench line, "settle the post-and-horizontal-line reticle on one target right after the other and squeeze the trigger. It was a lot like going to a carnival and shooting those little toy crows off the fence. *Bap!* The crow disappeared and you moved over to the next crow," Hamilton continued. "By the time you got to the end of the fence you came back to the beginning and the crows were all lined up again ready for you to start over. I don't know who the Chinese first sergeant was over there, but he kept throwing up another crow for me every minute or two."

Some other Americans joined Hamilton to point out targets and cheer as if they were at a shooting gallery at the county fair. Yet in the end there was tragedy for the Americans.

"The GIs never made it past the wire. Heavy Chinese mortar and artillery fire stopped the advance and started cutting the [American] infantry to pieces. The tanks scurried for cover when the artillery fire singled them out; they weren't much benefit on the steep grade anyhow." Hamilton recalled all this with more than a little bitterness. "By the time the GIs withdrew from the hill, dashing from rock to rock, demoralized and defeated my gun barrel was so hot to the touch that I could hardly touch it. You could smell the Cosmoline being cooked out of the metal." And yet, Hamilton himself had mitigated the loss with his rifle. "I know I shot at least forty Chinese before the attack bogged down and the enemy went back to their burrows. Bodies had to be stacked up in the Chinese trenches. I wondered if the first sergeant over there ever figured out what happened."

CHAPTER ELEVEN

Elephant Ears and White Feathers

There is no hunting like the hunting of a man,
and those who have hunted armed men long enough
And liked it never cared for anything else thereafter
— ERNEST HEMINGWAY

CARLOS, A DARK-HEADED, SKINNY MARINE WHO WORE SUNGLASSES anytime he could, was a champion. He had proved just that by winning the US one-thousand-yard High-Power Rifle Championship in October 1966 at Camp Perry, Ohio. Now, eighteen months later he gazed through a telescope sight down a hill toward rice paddies being navigated by a Vietnamese kid not yet thirteen on a bike. His spotter was also a marine sergeant. Neither the sniper nor his spotter Charlie wore shirts that hot, nearly windless day in February. Carlos Norman Hathcock crouched cross-legged just behind his M-2 .50-caliber machine gun equipped with a Unertl sniper scope. Some would say that the Unertl was the best scope around.

This kid was trouble. He carried at least four rifles, a haversack likely carrying rifle cartridges, and magazines. Volunteer or not, the kid had likely been recruited by the Vietcong (VC) to work as a resupply mule carrying armaments to an enemy patrol somewhere in the area. The Americans would likely spot them only after some poor marine had been shot in the back. It was decision time.

The kid was right below Carlos when the shot rang out, knocking this junior VC over his handlebars and into the orange dust, scattering his ammunition all around him. Carlos smiled for a minute, savoring how he had knocked the bike over instead of killing the kid, giving junior a chance to run away. Pity that he didn't take it. Instead, junior picked up one of the weapons and jammed in a banana-curved magazine for the umpteenth time. Hathcock knocked him down a second time before the weapon was in the air. This time junior didn't get up. What happened next was almost routine. A marine squad went down the hill to the paddies and picked up the weapons as Vietnamese farmers carried junior toward the nearby village.

Hathcock took all this in and pulled the dog-eared school assignment book out of his shirt pocket to take a few notes. Later, he prepared a formal situation report for his commanding officer. End of story, at least for now.

Hathcock and Roberts knew the routine as well as if they had been VC themselves. The Chinese shipped the weapons by railroad into Hanoi, where they were repacked and sent south via the Ho Chi Minh trail to wherever the VC needed them. The particular load came to I Corps, as the Americans called it, which stretched from the 17th parallel up to the most northernmost ridges of the Central Highlands.

Roberts and Hathcock were near Duc Pho, at the southern tip of the I Corps territory, high on a hill overlooking farms, mud-and-straw huts by the hundreds, and steep mountains to the west rising and falling into some of the best rice-farming land in the world.

Hathcock and Roberts went on with the task at hand, methodically scanning across "Indian Country" as the Americans called it, looking for anything suspicious, be it a woman with a bag that seemed just too big or a boy on a bike. The VC didn't honor too many limits where using civilians for warfare provided a ready advantage. He'd seen them use three-year-olds as booby traps placed strategically to draw the ready welcome of GIs carrying chocolates. Older Vietnamese children sometimes offered GIs cold sodas containing small pieces of broken glass mixed with ice.

What a war. And what a different place from the farm in the Greater Little Rock, Arkansas, Metroplex where he had grown up staying with his grandmother. Now in the 8th year of his Marine Corps career at age twenty-five, he looked forward to seeing his wife Josephine, who went by Jo and Sonny, their little boy, in a month or two.

First, however, the marines had to clear the Duc Pho area of VC. Carlos would be a big part of that, using his .50-caliber machine gun as a sniper weapon. Carlos invented this strategy for one simple reason: increased range. The machine gun offered a three thousand yard stable trajectory, one-3rd greater than his trusty .30-06 rifle.

Carlos waited for the morning cross-legged behind his machine gun as his commanding officer scanned the horizon for the VC who soon would be looking at American helicopters helping his battalion conduct a sweep through the area. Those who didn't want to stay and fight might try to cross through two or three football fields of flooded rice before Hathcock could knock them down. The VC called him White Feather because of the ornament he wore on his bush hat.

Three helicopters broke the early morning stillness just as a call for "Red Man" blared over the radio. "Tell them we're ready here," said the major, and so they were. Three CH-46 Sea Knight three-rotor helicopters followed ridge lines down to their landing zones as VC small arms began to chatter. Seconds later, the marines dropped on the ground were on their own, even as other helicopters landed to their west, blocking any errant VC hoping for a quick escape up the nearby mountains.

Hathcock already knew it would be minutes if not hours before he saw any action. The experienced VC in this valley were in trenches well protected and hidden by bushes and trees; getting them up and out during this sweep would take some time. Eventually, even the savviest among the veteran VC had no choice but to run. Hundreds would run for the last time this day. Two others tried a different tactic, low crawling through the brush right next to the submerged rice fields White Feather and the major were watching that morning. The VC duo heard Americans behind them and knew they had no choice but to stand and run. The major wanted them forced back into the sweep, but when Carlos placed a warning shot in the water just in front of them, they kept coming. "Kill them," said the major. Carlos shot them both within seconds, ending the gunfire in his section, at least for a while.

Soon Carlos spotted another target about 2,500 yards downhill, washing his face in the rice water, a Chinese rifle slung over his back. Hathcock shot him in the chin as the VC stood up. A few hours later the Duc Pho operation ended and Hathcock returned the machine gun to the weapons platoon, after putting the Unertl scope back on his .30-06 sniper rifle. He carried the rest of his equipment in a standard-issue North Vietnamese backpack that had one large compartment and several pouches, perfect for American snipers. Soon they boarded a twin-rotor helicopter for a quick trip back to Hill 55, their base of operation.

Seven years had passed since his mother signed the papers allowing Carlos to join the marines on his seventeenth birthday. Despite a skinny five foot ten frame, Carlos could lift his own weight over his head while shoveling concrete every work day since quitting high school at age fifteen. He arrived at the Marine Corp Recruit Depot (MCRD) in San Diego aboard the standard dirty, dull-gray bus that picked Carlos and some thirty other recruits up at Lindbergh field, eleven miles away. Thirteen weeks of hell began just before midnight.

Carlos went through scout/sniper school in Hawaii, won the Marine Pacific division rifle championship, and met his future wife in New Bern, North Carolina, nineteen miles north of the Marine Corps Air Station at Cherry Point. While at Cherry Point, he worked at the rifle range and became a national shooting champion.

Now eight years later, back at Hill 55 in I Corps, Hathcock thought through tomorrow's mission at nearby "Elephant Valley" just to their north. Lance Corporal John Roland Burke of Alabama would be spotting for him during this mission, which might last as long as a week, depending on how long their cans of peanut butter and cheese held out. That night, Carlos wrote a letter to Josephine back in North Carolina but didn't mention the morning mission. She thought that Carlos was still teaching other marines marksmanship, until the morning she read in the *Raleigh News and Observer* that the deadliest marine sniper in Vietnam was Carlos Hathcock, "a Scout-Sniper with the 1st Marine Division in Vietnam [who] earned praise from his commanding officer for 'making life miserable' for the Viet Cong." The article continued, saying that "Sgt. Carlos N. Hathcock of New Bern is one of several 'expert marksmen' credited with killing more than 65 enemies. Firing at ranges up to 1,125 yards, Hathcock and the 'crew' have been picking off better than two enemies a day, without a friendly casualty."

That morning Josephine read the article simmered in anger and wrote her husband a long angry letter. Virtually at the same time, "in-country" at his Vietnam station, Carlos closed his eyes in the evening darkness and thought about his twenty-fifth birthday.

After that, the months rolled by, bringing him closer and closer to his least known Vietnam exploit, against an enemy that was code-named Apache. This sniper was about five years older than Carlos, stood five feet tall with small pointed nose and widely set brown eyes, hinting at a dab of French ancestry.

Apache kept a three-by-five inch makeshift notebook made from scrap American packing materials bought in Hanoi while training to become intelligence operative and, almost as an afterthought, a sniper platoon commander. The assigned watch was Hill 55, the very place where Hathcock now lived when he wasn't killing VC and North Vietnamese Army (NVA) regulars. Apache found a good vantage point near several women wearing black silk blouses and straw hats laboring in a rice field. When they finished, Apache followed close behind as they returned to their village, peeling away when Apache reached the hut that hid a Russian M189/31 Mosin-Nagant 7.62×54 mm sniper rifle with a scope. Within minutes, Apache disappeared into the jungle.

Earlier, Captain Edward James Land, an intelligence officer, met with four men who just jumped out of a helicopter that brought them from Chu Lai to Hill 55 and a lieutenant who had been assigned to brief them. The six men met next to an empty tent that had been fitted with a dark green canvas cover, plywood, and pine walls, and large screen covered windows and doors.

Land wanted to know how soon this Da Nang quartet would be in action. The lieutenant jumped right into a briefing, telling the Da Nang four that Hill 55 was surrounded by one of the most active areas in Vietnam. Pulling a creased, well-worn map covered in plastic out of his trouser cargo pocket, he pointed out the two most prevalent trouble areas, Charlie Ridge and Happy Valley. He also pointed out other VC-infested areas, called Dodge City, Elephant Valley, and, worse still, Oklahoma Territory, just crawling with VC. Of course, that wasn't the term he used for the enemy soldiers. The lieutenant even had a recommendation, delivered in his own unique way, pointing to a particular spot on the worn-out map: "You could set up on finger four of this very hill, just out back of this hooch," he said, index fingering rice fields, hedgerows, and jungle overlooked by a small bunker a few feet away from the tent's rear screen door. The lieutenant remarked that they could probably "shoot off into that general area and probably kill or wound more VC than you ever saw down at Chu Lai." His excitement grew. "If you're huntin' Charlie, you've come to the right place—he lives down there."

By the time the lieutenant and Captain Land finished the briefing, Hathcock and the other snipers fresh in from Da Nang knew that Apache would be their first target. Somewhere among the huts surrounding the rice fields below Hill 55, Hathcock knew that Apache waited for him. Yet that was not quite accurate. The VC didn't live in the huts themselves but in a series of tunnels beneath the huts comprising the company headquarters of the VC sniper platoon that hunted marines. Later, the marines learned that the underground complex included the rooms one would expect, an ammunition bunker and sleeping chambers, but also some surprises. Those surprises included a well-equipped conference room and a hidden observation post.

All around the VC headquarters were booby-trapped tunnels. And it was there that Apache sat under a lantern, marking up a map spread out on a makeshift pine board table. Two VC watched as Apache consulted the makeshift notebook and wrote something on the map.

Just about then, six marines outfitted in bush hats and camouflage uniforms bounded onto a chopper already occupied by two 26th Marine Regiment companies ready for a three-day reconnaissance of a nearby muddy river and adjoining flood plain. These new snipers working with Hathcock included Gunnery Sgt. James Wilson, Lance Cpl. John Burke, Staff Sgt. Charles Roberts, and Master Sgt. Donald Reinke who would conduct a separate mission guarding the flanks of the main force. They followed Land to a large tent sporting lots of antennas and camouflage. The inside was dressed out with a huge plastic-covered map mounted on four-by-eight-foot plywood. Land had already devised a plan calling for three two-man teams strung out along the river bend, covering both the bend itself and flat wetlands on the opposite side of the river. The known VC positions were marked with red grease pencils. The six snipers would concentrate on known enemy emplacements on low hills overlooking the river flats. Hathcock couldn't contain himself. "Sir it looks like pretty good huntin' over there," he blurted out. The major in charge of the mission was more circumspect. "Could be, Hathcock. It just could be."

The major shared his worries about the danger of this mission, knowing that the VC might easily identify where the sniper fire was coming from. The problem was that in case of trouble there was no real cover to fight from, other than a single five-foot-high knoll behind some rice paddies.

And so Hathcock and the other five snipers hidden in tall grass with no real protecting ditches or other cover watched for VC across the river. They watched from prone positions in matted grass, over their rifles, and through their rifle scopes now and again. A flicker of light, just a flash, soon told him that someone was on the move, but not for long. Seconds later, a rifle shot rang out. A quick look with Land's binoculars revealed a soldier tangled in roots along the river, blood trickling down his back, a Chinese K-44 rifle still grasped in his hands.

The VC waited several hours to move again, but when they did Hathcock went into action, ignoring the sweat in the corner of his eye long enough to focus on a man in the middle of the column. Slowly, ever so slowly, he took the slack out of the trigger long enough to put around in his target's chest, just as Land, now in the action as well, tried to take out the VC point man, but hit him in the hip. The score so far was one KIA (killed in action) and one WIA (wounded in action) but now Land and Hathcock could hear more guns behind them. A few VC had somehow slipped by the pair, Americans on higher ground were counting coup. Within minutes, Land sent a green phosphorous flare into the air, signaling the other marines that it was time to meet at their rally point, wait until dark, and then return to the fire base.

While Land's snipers waited outside the operations tent, he discussed the next day's mission with the major in charge. Land was reluctant to repeat today's mission tomorrow for concern that the VC would anticipate just this and move in mortars or even rockets. His suggestion was worth considering. "I'd rather move on the hillside to the right. We can still cover that area. We will just have to shoot at a thousand yards instead of six hundred. And all my snipers are excellent thousand-yard shooters. Hathcock, as a matter of fact, is the United States champion at a thousand yards."

The major had a different point of view. He was skeptical about even the best of snipers being able to hit fast-moving targets more than half a mile away with the accuracy that would be needed tomorrow. "You'll miss more than you'll hit," said the major. Land made a single comment to the effect that going back to the same position a second day violated "all sniper doctrine that I have read or encountered" but in the end accepted the orders, asking only that some covering fire be prepared for tomorrow's mission. "We'll plot some targets on the hills above that flat," promised the major. "If you take fire, it will come from there. A pair of red stars will turn on the fireworks. Good luck, Captain." The snipers eavesdropped well enough to hear the outcome. "Do I need to explain anything to you men or did you get it all?" Land asked. He was not happy.

Years later, Hathcock remembered the following morning as the darkest he'd ever encountered during his sniping career. "The dark shapes of the bushes and grass blended with the sky," he recalled. His eyes strained trying to find contrast until at last some hilltops appeared "against the starless heavens."

During the morning hours, Hathcock thought about how right Captain Land had been; this might be his last day on earth, or so it seemed as he looked down at where the river ran, if only he could see it. Soon Hathcock himself moved out, sniffing along the way for the river smells that would tell him how far they had walked. Soon enough Hathcock, his partner, and two other sniping teams were looking at new daylight, listening to birds in the shallows, and all too soon faintly clanking metal downriver, clanking that became more pronounced as the seconds went by, seeming like minutes. Burke saw them first, aimed at a VC head, and fired, just as Hathcock did the same, before the familiar, almost comforting sounds of American Winchesters were drowned out by Chinese quad .51 fire combing through the bushes where the Americans hugged the ground. This wasn't return fire from the VC the snipers had targeted. Instead, quad .51 bullets mixed with red tracers showered down from the high hill ground they just left.

Captain Land yelled that it was time to get out of Dodge and sent two red-star signals into the air as the six snipers who reported to him ran for their lives. Master Sergeant Reinke fell behind, but he hadn't been hit. Reinke had fallen into a mud hole that sucked him in right to his armpits as .51 quad bullets rained in all around. The other guys had to pull so hard on his arms to get him out of the hole that they fell back onto the ground themselves once he was loose.

All the snipers had to do now was run for a low dike near the river and low crawl to some open grassland and rendezvous behind a low, protecting knoll, as marine mortar fire passed over them toward the VC positions in the hills above them. The only dry thing Hathcock had on him was a package of cigarettes. If only his hands would stop shaking long enough to light one.

The VC around Hill 55 were clever enough. Not long after Hathcock returned from that second river mission, he jumped to his feet after hearing a command-detonated explosion near the Hill just in time to watch a marine patrol running away from an ambush.

The VC knew that the Americans often used a trail cutting through a series of rice fields as a shortcut to the crossroads they regularly patrolled. This time the VC planted claymore mines all along the shortcut trail, detonated the explosives when the marines were most vulnerable, anticipated that the Americans would leap into the rice paddies for protection, and peppered them with rifle fire. Three dead and one wounded marines were left behind. Everybody at Hill 55 knew that the VC would now use them for bait, just as the Americans had before.

The major pressed Captain Land and his snipers for suggestions. Land had one: find the VC, let the American snipers take them out, and retrieve the four marines, including the one they could hear screaming all night. The next morning they watched the screaming survivor run toward them, blood gushing from where his private parts had been just a few minutes ago, before the female VC interrogator carved them out. The doomed man reached the American concertina wire, leaned against it, and died. Hathcock knew that what had to be done would have to wait.

Four days later, as he listened to B-52s in the far off distance drop loads on other enemies, Hathcock watched a lone man returning again and again to a hut near a tree line, without any farming tools or anything else in his hands, which would explain his behavior. The walls of monsoon rain that soon fell on Hathcock and the two other snipers pushed the suspected VC inside the hut for much of the afternoon. To Hathcock, he looked guilty as hell. That very day an NVA division general read a letter from the VC interrogator telling him about Hathcock. She called him "White Feather" and told the general about the new sniper school at Hill 55 and how effective their tactics had been in impairing the revolution. The old general listened to American bombs dropping dangerously close to the very place where he wrote a secret communiqué dealing with the American snipers.

That evening back at the clearing, Hathcock watched the suspected VC make his move, reaching just inside the hut door for something bulky, something that turned out to be an SKS military rifle. Seconds later, Hathcock squeezed the trigger and turned to the student who was serving as his sniper partner.

"Let's go home."

On the way back to the hill, they stopped to look at the dead VC, take his rifle, and pick up a white feather lying nearby, remembering the sea birds he watched flying toward the ocean just a few hours before.

After spending more time writing reports, sniper school lesson plans, and other paperwork than he cared for, Captain Land took White Feather back to a sniper hide about three miles from Hill 55 overlooking a clearing that the marines used for a landing zone. From the hide, they could see the junction of two trails frequently used by the marines themselves, but just as often by the VC. Today, they hoped to take out some VC soldiers and maybe even a sniper or two. Should they be extremely lucky, they would put their sights on the VC woman who tortured, emasculated, and murdered their friend.

The morning wore on without any action, until another sniper appeared about two hundred yards away, walking along a stream, carrying a bolt action rifle with a long, wooden stock. He wasn't wearing a marine uniform, so Hathcock and his commanding officer quibbled about who would take the kill. When the argument turned into a wrestling match over the rifle, the target heard them and disappeared into the bush.

They knew that the VC sniper would return with reinforcements. This seemed like an opportunity to Hathcock, who proposed staying until the escapee returned with more VC to kill, despite the danger of being outnumbered. Captain Land arranged for a marine patrol to cover their backsides. Those details attended to, Captain Land and Master Sergeant Hathcock moved to a different, higher position above the clearing to avoid being nailed where the escaping VC had last seen them. They also found a better hide with a wider view of the clearing.

Their hope was that the interrogator, who also commanded VC sniper operations in this area, would assume that Land and Hathcock were overconfident bozos who she could easily capture as prizes or kill if there was no other practical choice. Getting to their next sniper hide had not been easy. They slowly low-crawled along the edge of the clearing, through short palm trees and jungle debris into tall thick grass and colocasia, a leafy green plant cultivated in Asia for at least ten thousand years which the GIs in Vietnam called elephant ears. They found a small ridge beneath the elephant ears, which served as a perfect natural resting place for their rifles during this surveillance operation. The patrol behind them found a second natural ridge, slightly higher than Hathcock and Land were using.

The lucky sniper who escaped from Land and Hathcock had some difficulty convincing the commander who met him in the series of tunnels and underground rooms that served as the VC headquarters. She was the very VC who had tortured and emasculated the American marine and nicknamed Hathcock White Feather. She recognized what an excellent catch Land and Hathcock would make, but she had already scheduled an ambush operation for her troops that evening. Since her planned ambush was very close to where Hathcock and Land had been spotted, she planned to work them in.

The low plants and palms offered Land and Hathcock a great sniper hide with relative safety but buzzed with hundreds if not thousands of mosquitoes and other biting insects that thrived on the simmering heat and humidity. This was a virtual bathhouse that kept both men swiping the moisture away from their eyes, even as the tiniest of insects found refuge on their bodies wherever they could, even inside their ears, nostrils, and eyelids. The snipers risked exposing themselves to deadly fire each time they swatted a mosquito.

Captain Land decided sometime after noon that if no VC showed up by 1600 hours (4:00 p.m.), these two marines would call it a day. Hathcock had no complaints about this decision, but within a few minutes spotted something moving around some tree trunks up at the crest of a nearby hill. That something he spotted was dressed in black and crawled through the jungle mire toward them while juggling an AK-47.

"Don't shoot, Carlos. He ain't alone," whispered Captain Land, who immediately noticed that the figure was carrying an ordinary assault weapon rather than a sniper rifle and figured this man was a scout. Maybe he was even sent by the woman VC they were hunting for, the VC that Hathcock thought about night and day. Captain Land served as Master Sgt. Hathcock's one-man support group that day, telling him, "Don't go gettin' your hopes up. It's likely we won't get a clear shot at her, even if we see her. And don't forget, she hit An Hoa last night, and that is way over the other side of Hill 55 from where we are now. She could just as likely be lying back there now, looking to catch herself another young boy to skin."

The VC scout crawled around through downed trunks and jungle rot for more than an hour, which assured Land and Hathcock that he was no doubt a scout who left the enemy underground complex two hours or so ahead of his unit, looking for American ambushers and snipers, After the VC thoroughly scouted the area, he disappeared over a hill, if only because that was just how Land and Hathcock wanted this situation to play out.

Not that they hadn't talked about killing him. Yet in the end they let him get away, hoping to bring in a whole stringer full of fish. Hathcock looked up at that November sky at 5:30 p.m., wondering how much longer Captain Land would let them wait for the lady VC, under a sun that had changed from bright white to a burning orange ball.

Within seconds, Master Sgt. Hathcock was begging Captain Land to wait for a few more minutes, minutes, as it turned out, that they didn't need. While Hathcock was mid-sentence, Land himself spotted a barely visible silhouette slink out of the shadows at the top of the hill. Better yet, within a few seconds, another one squatted to the left of the first figure. The VC commanding officer that the marines now called Apache had arrived.

Land was sure this was her because he had seen photos and sketches in the files of the marine intelligence officer back at the division command post on Hill 55. Land thought through his options and decided that artillery offered the best chance of taking her out.

The first round took out three of the seven VC on the patrol, sending another two toward Land and Hathcock, while their commanding officer fell on her face near the point of impact. She wasn't down long. She bounced up and scrambled away in a panic, toward Land and Hathcock, as fate would have it, maybe remembering that she'd had trouble on this little hill before. After all, this had been her headquarters before the American bombers came. She didn't hear the VC scout running behind her, yelling with everything he had for her to stop running directly toward the Americans. By the time she turned around toward the scout, Hathcock had her chest in his sights. Turning away from the Americans only assured that his first shot hit her in the spine. His second shot into what was left of her ripped through her shoulder and lungs, leaving Hathcock plenty of time to drop the VC scout before he could scurry away.

All in a day's work.

Chapter Twelve

Long Shot

Joe LeBleu proudly claimed an American military heritage dating back to the revolution. More recently, his great uncle Ernie Simpson, a member of Darby's Rangers during World War II, claimed to have raided Mussolini's castle and killed two Italians who had captured and intended to kill him. How were they to know that Simpson could understand Italian?

Joe himself received an honorable discharge from the 1st Battalion, 75th Ranger Regiment six months before 9/11. He was standing in Manhattan when the planes went into the World Trade Center, taking down both towers before his very eyes. The following March, he attended funeral services for buddies killed during Operation Anaconda in Afghanistan. After one such funeral in Jacksonville, Florida, both sides of the street on the way to the cemetery were filled with men, women, and children wearing red, white, and blue T-shirts. Banners expressing support for America's defenders could be seen even into the far distance along the sides of the roads.

LeBleu's old teammates Sergeant Bradley Crose, Corporal Marc Anderson, and Corporal Matthew Commons were killed in the effort to rescue US Navy SEAL Neil Roberts, who was executed by al-Qaeda. While driving to Savannah, Georgia, after the service, LeBleu decided to become a US Army Ranger once again. Six months later, he resolved to become a sniper. The reasons might be complicated, but during his previous Ranger service, he had sensed that something had been missing. During his second tour of service, he wanted to penetrate enemy lines and rely solely upon his own skills rather than relying on others for the furtherance of the mission.

Eventually, he became the legend called "Long Rifle," the title of the LeBleu memoir which is the primary source for this chapter. That destiny wasn't apparent to LeBleu or anyone else when he arrived at the US Army Sniper School in Fort Benning, Georgia, on July 5, 2003. He knew that this was one of, if not, *the* toughest schools in the US Army. Rumor had it that the instructors here took the trainees to the point of physical exhaustion on a regular basis. LeBleu joined Class 502-03 as "Roster Number 11," in gambling terms, Snake Eyes, the slang assigned to rolling two ones in dice.

He quickly learned that most candidates were weeded out of sniper school during the very first week of rigorous physical fitness tests. Those that survived moved on to basic rifle skills tests with the M24 7.62×51mm sniper rifle and a full week of classroom instruction from the *US Army Sniper Training Field Manual* balanced out by training on how to operate a sniper scope and make your own "ghillie" suit.

Scots gamekeepers had invented the ghillie to disguise themselves and fit into virtually any surrounding. The arcane sixteenth-century Scottish Gaelic term literally means lad or servant. Eventually, lowland Scots used the term to insult followers of Highland Chiefs. How the term became associated with camouflage suits is simply unknown. British Lovat Scouts first used ghillie suits during World War I. The Ranger training regimen called for the prospective snipers to spend part of each training day in a "ghillie Shack making their own ghillie suits and pulling maintenance on their sniper equipment." During those early days, Army Rangers at sniper school began firing their weapons daily at ranges from two hundred to seven hundred yards. Once the trainers were convinced that the students were all competent with iron sights, the training transitioned to the Leupold 10× sights then often used in combat missions. The first week also included training focused on mental stress to eliminate those candidates most likely to drop out later in the program. After learning the "nuts and bolts" of sniping in week two, the trainees moved on to such arcane subjects as "Kentucky windage," which is to say, developing the skills necessary to estimate wind speed and the range of the target through sheer gut instinct. No one got out of sniper school unless the candidate could hit at least 70 percent of stationary metal targets from various ranges using M24 rifles. The candidates also had to draw sketches of topographic and panoramic targets, the latter being what a person sees right in front of them. Topographic target sketches reflect a bird's eye view.

Of course there were written exams, covering practical subjects as well as sniper history. Moving from academic to practical in those last few weeks, the candidate snipers had to show the instructors their stalking skills, demonstrate how to set up a sniper hide in the bushes with minimal movement, and move as far as eight hundred meters to set up a firing position, all while wearing a cumbersome, uncomfortable ghillie suit.

The Final Shot test required the candidate sniper to shoot two rounds at a target placed somewhere between six hundred and one thousand meters away within three minutes, calculating the necessary windage and elevation before firing. Those candidates who didn't pass the final shot test were recycled, which is to say they had to take the whole course all over again.

LeBleu passed the Final Shot test the first time and immediately received orders for Western Iraq. After a brief vacation back home with his wife and buddies in Fayetteville, North Carolina, he prepared his gear and arrived in Fallujah, Iraq, on Sunday, September 7, 2003. Later, he remembered the place smelling like buffalo manure, goat droppings, diesel fumes, and raw sewage.

He joined Attack Company, 1st Battalion, 32nd Regiment, 10th Mountain Light Infantry and soon became the "go to" guy for an assortment of intelligence gathering, reconnaissance, and sniper missions. After all, he was the only former US Army Ranger with prior experience. The situation was grim or challenging depending on a soldier's perspective. In LeBleu's estimation, Fallujah was the very heart of Iraqi insurgent and al-Qaeda terrorist activity. Many other professional military officers agreed with him. After all, the US Central Command (CENTCOM) designated Fallujah as the most dangerous city in all of Iraq.

During the next seven months, LeBleu worked missions night and day and if truth be told, loved every minute of it, even when those assignments took him to the dry sands of Kuwait. September 2003 found LeBleu starting his first combat mission as a paratrooper sniper, telling himself, of all things, that "this should be fun." When his C-130 touched down among the heat mirages and sand dunes at Al Taqaddum Air Force Base, he quickly learned that his new outfit, Task Force 1 Panther did not have an active intelligence section. And so, snipers like LeBleu had no one to turn to for hard detailed information about the geographic features, terrain or culture, common heights of the male population, standard window, and door measurements so critical for successful operations.

LeBleu and the other snipers had to rely upon their training and instincts to fulfill those early missions. His spotter, Specialist Steve Eggleston, a quiet, blond paratrooper from Los Angeles, had already served a year in Afghanistan. Relying on his prior extensive combat experience, Team Leader LeBleu briefed and trained Eggleston and other scouts in his unit on what to look for in their upcoming missions. His own three-man sniper team, consisting of sniper, spotter, and radio man was then somewhat uncommon in the US Army. LeBleu and Eggleston were supported by Private First Class Arroyo, a lean six-footer also from Los Angeles who lugged the radio for the team. Officially, Arroyo was a radio transmission operator or "RTO" who would also carry an M4/M203 assault rifle/grenade launcher. LeBleu later described Arroyo as having hawk-like features, with dark eyes, short black hair, and a quick-witted sharpness second to no soldier LeBleu ever met. "I never had to tell him anything twice," LeBleu later recalled, which was important in that first mission on Monday, September 8, 2003.

He recalled that "operating in a desert environment in the Near East in that kind of heat can be difficult, but it is nearly overwhelming when you're carrying sixty-plus pounds of gear. Sweat dripped from our eyes and immediately began soaking our uniforms; the sauna-like heat was nearly choking on that late summer day in Western Iraq." Here the temperatures reaching 125 to 140 degrees Fahrenheit in Fallujah in early September 2003 made it challenging, especially when there was no way to escape it. Even their drinking water was usually warm or even hot.

Sergeant First Class Richard Lopez, the platoon sergeant who ordered LeBleu and his team into combat that morning, was not much on talk but big on action. "Load up and roll," his voice boomed into the hootch. During a previous life, he'd been in the marine infantry. Rumor had it that not long after enlisting in the 101st Airborne at Fort Campbell, Kentucky, he'd ordered one of his men to remove a gold earring. When the man refused, Lopez ripped it out explaining that only pirates and cheerleaders wore earrings and the soldier in question was neither.

Arroyo, Eggleston, and several others got to the Humvee before LeBleu. Since everyone else was already loaded up in the cargo area, fitted with Kevlar helmets, body armor, and vertical magazine pouches, LeBleu, being the last man there, had to drive. This "naked" Humvee carried no armor beneath, on the sides, or anywhere else. This left the team totally exposed to the firepower that might come their way, not to mention the landmines that the Humvee might trigger traveling down the road to their mission. LeBleu and his passengers traveled 3rd in the vehicle convoy, past all the hootches and out the gate into the burning hot morning.

The very first Task Force 1 Panther mission in Fallujah this morning took them out to the intersection of Highways 1 and 10, which the American planners dubbed the Cloverleaf but should have been named IED Central given the number of improvised explosive devices (IEDs) encountered there. LeBleu scanned the surroundings as he drove, "taking mental photographs of the city and remembering key landmarks, such as mosques, how the apartments and buildings were set up, how staircases would lead up to the rooftops and whether there were fire escapes on houses and buildings." He also noted how many people were on the streets, how they were dressed, while looking for suspicious eye movements, pistols, knives, and anything else signaling immediate danger.

After all, "given that it was everybody's first mission in Fallujah, you could feel the tension all around you, like a cloud hanging over all of us. Even though there was nothing but sun that morning, that cloud was damn sure there." LeBleu scanned and collected data as they drove along. When they came to the end of one dusty street, "I noticed a group of Iraqi men all wearing their red *khaffiyehs* [a form of scarf] ninja style, wrapped completely around their heads and face, with only their eyes exposed."

Watching their "cold death stares," LeBleu made a mental note about *red headdresses on groups of men*. Seconds later, the convoy came to the end of the street and turned left. "As my vehicle was turning left, our convoy suddenly disappeared into smoke. Dazed and confused, I had no idea what had just happened. I didn't realize I had just been through my first IED ambush."

At first all LeBleu could hear was the ringing of his own ears, but squealing brakes and screeching tires soon drowned that out. LeBleu thought at first that he had lost his legs, since he was covered by street concrete but knew better when they began to throb in pain. The convoy had been struck by an IED composed of at least three 155 mm artillery rounds wrapped in detonation cord and probably some plastic explosives for good measure. One thing for sure: the convoy was right in the middle of a coordinated ambush.

He shouted to the 10th Mountain soldiers in front of him to move, move, move, "none of us knowing if the driver in front of us was dead or alive as the vehicle just sat there. I pulled around the immobile Humvee with my snipers laying down heavy suppressive counterfire. As I wheeled around it, in the same motion I grabbed an M4 with my right hand. Throwing the rifle over my left arm for leverage with my left hand on the wheel, I began returning fire while evasively driving us out of the kill zone." LeBleu kept returning fire to his left where they were getting hit hard from telltale muzzle flashes flaming from an alley. "I emptied a magazine rapidly, shooting single shots. Clearing the kill zone, I yelled back, 'Changing mags!' McGuire [another sniper] laughed when he heard me shout that I was changing magazines, because it's something you should never hear your driver say in combat."

"My magazines were doubled, which is slang for taping or joining two mags together, for fast reloading. Somehow, by the grace of God, I was able to hit the magazine release button on my M4 with my right hand while keeping my left hand on the wheel." LeBleu made sure the mags fell on his lap, grabbed them with his right hand, and inserted the fresh magazines. "Meanwhile, the bolt had locked to the rear as with all M4s, so I turned my M4 sideways, pushed the rifle forward very hard so that the bolt release hit my forearm, and chambered a new round." He yelled, "I'm up!" to let his snipers know that he had reloaded. "McGuire laughed again. I looked back now and could see Warner standing up with the .50 caliber Barrett sniper rifle shouldered, scanning the windows and rooftops left to right, looking south-totally focused, but, nevertheless, an easy target for the enemy."

Now the Humvee LeBleu was driving was the second vehicle in the convoy. Later, LeBleu remembered yelling to the men in the vehicle behind him, trying to find out whether any of the 10th Mountain guys were killed or wounded. Whatever the condition of the men inside the vehicles, the convoy began rolling, a good sign. They moved up the road about a mile and stopped, staggering the Humvees on each side of the road in a "herringbone" formation, just as Iraqi vehicles began approaching the kill zone.

"Welcome to Iraq, boys. That was one hell of a welcoming party." LeBleu was laughing when he said this, but this wasn't a random remark. He learned in his previous service that this kind of joking relieved tension and helped soldiers focus on the challenges they faced. Soon enough LeBleu and the others learned that two 10th Mountain soldiers were wounded by shrapnel, were rapidly losing blood, and had to be treated as soon as possible. The entire convoy turned around, sped through Fallujah past Camp Volturno, which the Americans had established on the outskirts of town, and on to Forward Operating Base St. Mere, three miles to the east. They arrived in time to save both men.

During the rest of September, LeBleu and his team conducted reconnaissance patrols just outside Fallujah. Typically, LeBleu carried an M24 sniper rifle and a 9 mm Beretta sidearm. "Jumping the wall" to go on missions at Volturno wasn't difficult at all since the hootch LeBleu's team slept in was right next to the compound wall. These missions were conducted around the clock.

LeBleu was the only available sniper with significant Delta Force mission experience. After three intense weeks, LeBleu was nominated for a Bronze Star with Valor insignia. During this series campaign, LeBleu gathered intelligence on suspected insurgents who wore red scarves and provided what he found to army intelligence, designated "S-2."

September drifted into October, bringing insurgent mortar and rocket attacks nearly every evening, typically beginning by 6:30 p.m. and ending within an hour. Mid-month a US Army Special Forces major sought him, complimented LeBleu as the "go-to sniper in this neck of the woods," and handed LeBleu a case containing an SR-25 7.62-caliber sniper rifle, very similar to one he had trained on as a Ranger over a decade before.

"Happy hunting," said the major, before he turned around and left. LeBleu quickly learned that this was no coincidence. The next day, LeBleu learned that he would be going out on a "leader's recon," military jargon for a reconnaissance carried out by the sniper team leader, the platoon sergeant, squad leaders, and others in key leadership positions. Soon enough, LeBleu confirmed his role in the reconnaissance with his commanding officer.

Captain Scott Kirkpatrick was a marathon runner who could run two miles in nine minutes. The mission would kick off the next morning at 8:00 a.m. On his way back to the sniper hootch inside Camp Volturno, the sky began to rain mortar rounds. Once the storm was over LeBleu returned to the hootch, briefed his men, and spent the night preparing for the next day.

Going over the infiltration route on his map of Fallujah, LeBleu made sure that he had every single detail down, refreshing his memory with measurements on everything that was specific to terrorists and insurgents and insurgents in Fallujah. He memorized the route of the leader's (reconnaissance), eyeballing the area between the southern edges of the city and the Euphrates River. He already knew about "the Boneyard," a place "filled with looted, stripped-down buildings that from a distance looked like whalebones and dinosaur skeletons. High green seas of saw grass jutted along both shores of the Euphrates, beyond the bone yard as water buffalo grazed in swampy grass fields nearby," LeBleu recalled.

"The bone yard was a strange ghosted place. It was a bare, eerie wasteland of looted factories. There were a few villages in close proximity and along with the water buffalo you'd see donkeys and goats meandering about." He remembered that it was not unusual to see dead goats near a dam south of the bone yard, on either side of a concrete bridge spanning the Euphrates.

Before he went to bed that night he "slipped my map into the left cargo pocket of my desert bottoms and walked outside, staring at the night sky. I was mentally preparing myself to be back in combat, even though I knew it was only a leader's [reconnaissance]. I remember telling myself 'Here we go.' Round two, back into the eye of the hurricane."

LeBleu woke up the next morning to "the fragrant odor of Fallujah," gathered his men, and headed to the 8:00 a.m. mission launch from the commanding officer's hootch. Once there, LeBleu jumped into the very back of the Humvee so that he would have sufficient elevation, when standing, to scan ahead of their convoy. LeBleu noticed that his driver put his M4 carbine next to him on the right, a lesson learned from the ambush they were in when LeBleu arrived earlier that September. Then they moved out into the hot, choking heat that was Fallujah, moving along dirt roads away from the Cloverleaf, as LeBleu, former US Ranger that he was, began taking mental pictures of the key mosques and other buildings they passed along the way. He could feel the tension and smell the ever-present stench of goat manure and human sewage. What a morning.

Although LeBleu had been in country less than a month, he'd already developed that sixth sense that warns experienced combat veterans that something was about to happen. This was more than the usual hateful stares from the locals as they drove through town. This was a distinct impression that they would be under fire soon. This was an impression that shook LeBleu by the shoulders and forced him to look at every pile of trash or huddle of suspicious-looking people the convoy passed as it sped through intersections. Another key indicator was empty streets or empty alleys, either of which usually meant a fight was coming; it was only a question of how soon.

They rolled on toward the bone yard, moving along the southernmost edge of Fallujah, positioned second in the convoy behind another Humvee outfitted with a mounted .50-caliber machine gun, which was well-matched with the MK19 40 mm grenade launcher in LeBleu's own vehicle. This was when LeBleu realized what he'd left behind. "Sweat was pouring and I remember thinking, *I hope we're not out here too much longer because I didn't bring any water.*" Long before this LeBleu had trained himself to survive for long periods in the desert without water, but not in weather this hot. "We snaked back onto the main dirt road leading to the Boneyard," he recalled, "away from the mud huts and concrete villas that we'd just passed. As we started to pull away from the village on the main dirt road, I scanned ahead through the clouds of dust to ensure we were still on our route."

He could see trouble maybe five hundred meters west, in the form of a white pickup truck coming from the south, rolling slowly through the crowds on both sides of a dirt road, heading north.

LeBleu now noticed that the lead Humvee in the convoy was pulling out too far ahead of them. He yelled out ordering the driver to close the fifty meters between the lead Humvee and LeBleu's own vehicle positioned second in the convey. The moment his own driver punched the accelerator to catch up, everything in LaBleu's world became blackness and smoke. The back of his own Humvee lifted off the ground, throwing him forward and into another man's back.

Staying up all night planning every contingency now paid off. "Somehow I pulled myself together quickly, got my bearing and dropped down, taking a knee in the back of the Humvee, dropping my chin to rest as the shock and blast of the IED slammed the Humvee back down on the dirt and into the dust thick in the air."

For reasons LeBleu himself didn't fully understand, he ended up kneeling over his sniper scope. "I know of no reason why I did this," he said later, "but I guess it was a gut feeling. One of my instincts as always, If you protect your glass (scope) you will always be able to see your target."

His ears were ringing harder and louder than they had from any other IED blasts. And this one felt ten times stronger than usual to him. "What seemed an eternity was probably only about thirty seconds, just enough time for me to get my bearings back." When he regained consciousness, he quickly started scanning 360 degrees, looking for a triggerman. He knew from field intelligence that "there would always be triggermen at least 300 meters from any IED ambush site. Once I'd completed my quick 360-degree scan, I turned to my team, to make sure they weren't wounded or dead."

While looking through the black smoke rising around them, LeBleu spotted a massive crater where the insurgents had placed, as LeBleu confirmed later, three "daisy-chained" 155 mm artillery rounds as the IED. This placement pointed out how clever the insurgents were becoming. They had embedded this IED in the road and then completely repaved over it.

After the convoy turned around, a hostile crowd began to gather to the west of the Americans, some three hundred meters away, even as a white pickup truck with men in the back carrying AK-47 assault rivals broke away from the hostiles, heading north. There was no gunfire yet, but the crowd began silently moving toward the Americans, many of them wrapped in the black or red khaffiyehs that hostiles often wore, but LeBleu had a plan. After receiving permission from one of the officers, he took a shot at one of the buildings just behind the crowd, spraying brown concrete on them, and sending them running in all directions. "Holy shit, nice shot," said the lieutenant, but LeBleu wasn't done. He could see movement on the rooftops and in some of the alleys northwest of the convoy, which turned into massive

AK-47 fire seconds later pouring into the American convoy from all points of the compass.

LeBleu saw an opportunity in all this chaos. A large yellow crane stripped of its tracks positioned about one hundred meters to the northwest could be used as a makeshift sniper hide. From here, they could support 10th Mountain infantry squads that then could advance to a nearby dirt berm and engage the hostiles. The enemy fire coming into the convoy now was massive but ineffective. Ordinarily, LeBleu would do a series of three second advances, diving for cover only long enough to avoid becoming a target, but this wasn't an ordinary combat situation. There was no cover whatsoever between him and the crane, one hundred meters away, so he would be in the open all the way there. LeBleu decided to have some fun as he stepped onto death's door. "Hey Robi," LeBleu said to a buddy, "You want to see something crazy?" He recalled this dangerous stunt years later. "I looked at him, said 'Watch this!' and leapt over the side of the Humvee with my rifle in my right hand and a small field radio tucked into my vest. I landed on both feet as the enemy fire increased, kicking up rounds in the dirt around me. I sprinted fast and hard, running first at about a 30-degree angle north and then aiming straight for the crane."

He could hear enemy fire from all sides and the shouts of 10th Mountain soldiers behind him. He remembered thinking, *damn, it's hot.* Soaked with sweat, closing in on the crane, Kalashnikov fire cracking next to him, he had never run faster.

"Somehow, by the grace of God, I made it," LeBleu remembered, with a sigh of relief. "I got down behind the back side of the crane, breathing heavily, trying to catch my breath. I took one deep breath and let it out, trying to calm myself down. I got into the prone position and crawled underneath the crane so that I'd have cover above me. As I was lying under the crane, I realized I didn't have good enough elevation to engage the rooftops." Since the tracks were off the wheels of the crane, he wedged himself between the body and the top of the track, while lying on the left wheel. Bullets were hitting the crane, ricocheting in all directions.

The improved line of sight allowed LeBleu to begin engaging insurgents on nearby rooftops. Soon he scoped a single figure firing an AK-47 at the Americans and dropped him out of action with his 3rd round. During a lull, he radioed his 10th Mountain brothers and gave Specialist Patrick Lybert, or someone with a similar voice, the all clear to move up beyond the crane to a dirt berm fifty meters in front of LaBleu. By then of course the insurgents had spotted him.

"I thought it would be best for me to stay put, and keep scanning for, and killing more enemy. I stayed under the crane, snug between the wheel and the body, as enemy rounds continued slamming into the crane [above him], thudding off the metal in an odd rhythm: first a few would hit, equally spaced, followed by a barrage of bullets hitting the crane all at once." He told himself that he would stay until he could hear the 10th Mountain coming up from the rear. They knew he was hiding somewhere around the crane, but they didn't know exactly where he was inside the crane. He heard about a squad of them quickly pass the crane, moving quickly to the dirt berm. Safety conscious even now, he dropped the barrel down so that he wouldn't be pointing at their backs. What he did next seems rather strange.

"I located and grabbed my three expended brass because first, a sniper should never shoot more than three rounds from one position. And second, you should never leave brass in combat as a sniper, in order to prevent the enemy from counter-tracking you." LeBleu tucked the three expended brass into a small pocket he'd fashioned on the left forearm sleeve of his blouse, slipped out of his hide, got under the crane, then slid out backward, keeping the crane between himself and the enemy. Coming out on one knee, LeBleu changed radio channels and called Martin, his spotter. "Do you see the dirt berm at your two o'clock?" LeBleu asked. "Meet me there."

"Roger," Martin replied.

And with that, LeBleu tucked his radio into his vest and joined the rest of the 10th Mountain squadron at the dirt berm for more shooting at insurgents on the rooftops. LeBleu scouted the enemy positions within view and decided that in the minutes that followed, his main concentrate of effort would be a paved road, running north to south in the distance. That very road would likely become the enemy avenue of approach if this skirmish turned into a battle. They knew that the Fallujah insurgents more often than not used the cargo areas of pickup trucks as gun platforms. In Africa, such trucks were called "Technicals" because they were often procured at the expense of naive nongovernmental organizations (NGOs) whose management assumed that the trucks would be used to distribute food and materials to the poor. Here in Iraq, such trucks were often fitted out with heavy machine guns. Both LeBleu and Martin now focused on a point in the road some eight hundred meters away. LeBleu now saw his objective as killing anyone approaching on the road toward the 10th Mountain, regretting all the time that there were not more snipers available. Since this operation started as a leadership reconnaissance, he was the only sniper here. There was another complication arising from the nature of this mission. He didn't have the spotting scope or the binoculars that were used to see beyond the range viewable through his sniper scope. The problem was mitigated by the Leupold 10× fixed scope on his SR-25 rifle. The Leupold gave him visibility out to 1,500 meters. Later, LeBleu remembered promising himself that he wouldn't be going on any more missions of any kind without a spotting scope. But for now LeBleu had to rely upon "Kentucky windage" and the range estimation training he had received during sniper school. Fortunately for LeBleu, a certain quiet had descended on the dirt berm as the hostile gunfire dropped from heavy to next to nothing in a matter of minutes.

LeBleu described this later. "A strange quiet descended all around us, and the 10th Mountain soldiers on the berm began changing magazines and drinking water. Everyone's uniform was dark with sweat and we were all red-faced and baked from the desert sun." LeBleu had the complete attention of his chain of command. "Fire team leaders were checking rounds and water on each soldier and the light machine gunners were reporting to their fire team leaders, who then reported up to their squad leaders."

Within a few minutes somebody called out for him, so he grabbed his rifle, hustled to another position behind the berm, drank some water, and began scanning from south to west, looking for opportunities.

While he was scoping the desert in front of him, the soldier next to him spotted a guy on a red motorcycle coming up the road. LeBleu knew that the insurgent in charge of placing IEDs in the roads to kill Americans in this area rode just such a motorcycle.

"Turning right, I scoped the road and could see the man on the red motorcycle, with a red *khaffiyeh* wrapped turban-style around his head." The man was wearing a white long flowing dishdasha. LeBleu inspected him carefully, trying to see if he had a cell phone, a weapon, or a package—anything out of the ordinary:

"He was about 75 meters away, approaching the crowd west of us and at that moment, I thought, *he's more than likely headed into Fallujah.* I told the 10th Mountain soldier 'He's got nothing on him' and then I heard my name shouted from the berm. I could tell it was Martin [LeBleu's spotter]. I sprang up and sprinted back to the berm. As I approached, someone from 10th Mountain began shouting, 'That's the white truck-that's the white truck!!'"

While running back to the dirt berm, LeBleu realized that this was the same suspicious white truck he had seen just before the IED ambush and began thinking through wind and distance as he looked around for Martin. Then, after getting in a prone position, he set his Leupold scope elevation to eight hundred meters. He didn't have time to find a better firing position. All he could do was look at the truck now traveling no faster than twenty-five miles an hour toward a factory in the bone yard about a mile away from him. LeBleu guessed that this truck would be loading up with insurgent reinforcements, AK-47s, an RPG (rocket-propelled grenade) launcher, and a heavy machine gun or two, complementing the four insurgents carrying AK-47s who were already in the large bed of the truck.

LeBleu quickly picked his first target, a tall, broad-shouldered insurgent standing up in the back of the truck, holding an AK-47. Martin spotted for him but didn't have that much to do. All LeBleu needed now was permission from the platoon leader who had just asked whether anyone had a shot on the white truck. He remembered what happened next. "I yelled out 'I've got it,' and I heard 'Take the shot.' That's all I needed to hear." LeBleu was tracking the white pickup truck as the sun reflected from the barrels of their Kalashnikovs. The driver was wearing a white *dishdasha* and a grayish-white turban. The passenger [inside the truck] wore a dark blouse with no *khaffiyeh*. He had short, greasy black hair. He looked fairly young, perhaps in his late teens. Two insurgents were squatting down in the bed of the pickup near the tailgate. They wore dark *dishdashas* and their barrels were sticking straight up from their legs. LeBleu now got ready to take some shots. "Bore-sighted now, I could see sunlight gleaming off their muzzles. My target was clad in a dark shirt and gray trousers, and also had no headdress. He had his right hand on the trigger of his AK-47, the Kalashnikov still shouldered, at the ready." LeBleu could see the wavy dark grains in the wood of his stock. To his left, an insurgent was in a black *dishdasha*—his AK now disappeared within his man dress, his left hand jammed into his body. Later, LeBleu remembered thinking, *none of them are wearing headdresses*, filing that key bit of field intelligence away for future use.

LeBleu knew that since the pickup was moving along at twenty to twenty-five miles per hour, he would have to give this target a significant lead. His spotter had the same idea and urged LeBleu to "give it daylight," meaning lead the target. LeBleu breathed once, told Martin he was about to take the shot, and did just that.

"With my index finger on the trigger, the metal touching the meaty portion between the tip and first bone joint, I slowly but steadily pulled the trigger to the rear. Conscious of my breathing and exhaling slowly, I pulled the trigger, sending my first round toward the pickup." Just after firing the first round, LeBleu saw dirt kick up just before the road and realized that it fell short. The white pickup truck rolled on, passengers unharmed and unaware of any immediate danger, cruising at the same speed.

LeBleu estimated that he was at least two hundred meters short. "*Holy cow, how far away is this?*" he thought, understanding that the target was considerably more than eight hundred meters away now. "The pickup truck was easily halfway to the looted factory in the Boneyard, insurgents in the back, their rifles held close. I was still zeroed in; I'd never taken my eye off the glass. My target continued to keep his Kalashnikov shouldered."

Without taking his eyes off of the target, LeBleu twisted the elevation knob on his scope, just as he heard Martin, his spotter, call out, "one thousand meters." Breathing quickly, he exhaled. "Very slowly now," LeBleu said later, "I applied pressure to the trigger, pulling it back, and I sent my second shot. I kept my follow-through, holding my trigger to the rear now, following the pickup through the scope. I saw the round hit the insurgent below the stock of his rifle, about midsection, on his right side. He dropped and fell backwards into the bed of the pickup, his Kalashnikov falling into the road."

The two remaining insurgents in the truck bed dropped their weapons and, when the truck screeched to a halt, threw their dead buddy out onto the ground as two more insurgents ran out of an alley and joined them. Now the truck peeled off in the direction of the factory as if nothing had happened. LeBleu wondered why the rest of the 10th Mountain guys didn't open up with the .50-caliber machine gun, but he kept his eye on the truck, watching it disappear into the distance.

Two women appeared to drag the body away. LeBleu had checked for breathing just a few minutes earlier and confirmed that the insurgent was dead. Now, almost casually, he looked at his elevation and realized that he'd killed this insurgent at a recorded distance of 1,100 meters.

And that was the longest recorded sniper shot in the Iraq War.

CHAPTER THIRTEEN

Luck Shot

MOST AMERICANS KNOW THE STORY OF CHRIS KYLE, THE TEXAS cowboy turned sniper, coauthor, and the subject of the book *American Sniper*, the primary source for this chapter and the subject of the later film. That said, few know the details of his last tour in Iraq and his exploits in Sadr City, a neighborhood of Baghdad, Iraq. Kyle spent his fourth and last deployment in Iraq and much of April 2008 in rat-infested slums that turned out to be an insurgent hellhole.

Midnight in Sadr City brought tense times patrolling through some of the most dangerous streets in Iraq, as more than a few dogs barked at the Americans. All Kyle could do, at least in this stage of the operation, was scan every corner of the street through his night vision equipment, hoping against hope that the next few minutes would not bring a barrage of bullets or, worse, an IED.

This was not a random foot patrol; instead, Kyle and his team were on their way to a specific drab-brown building to check out some suspicious circumstances. They didn't knock on the door. Instead, they prepared to breach a metal grate in front of the door as someone inside appeared, claimed he didn't have a key to let them in, and ran for the second floor as they broke down the door. The good news was that the first two floors were empty, but just as Kyle started into a room on the 3rd floor, the whole place blew up. Kyle thought at first that someone on his team had thrown a frag (fragmentation grenade) into the room, but they learned that one of the neighbors or, more likely, an insurgent had lobbed an RPG (rocket-propelled grenade) into the house. And now the hostile gunfire began ricocheting and piercing through the flimsy walls of this dump, as Kyle yelled out the order that might save at least some of them.

"Out of the house!" he yelled and later remembered that just as the last of the Americans cleared the house an extraordinarily large IED exploded down the street, knocking more than a few of them off their feet. The Americans regrouped, ran to another building, and prepared to blow their way in just as gunfire from every direction poured in, even from above them.

Kyle wondered once again whether this would be his last night on earth. A month ago he was getting ready to conduct long-range desert patrols, but first they had to build their own base camp, guided by a few "Seabees," Naval Construction Battalion ("C B") experts. One morning Kyle's chief woke him up with the news: Kyle and a number of other snipers were now assembling for a special operation. Sadr City, a suburb that housed some two million Shiites, was the domain of an intensely anti-Western cleric for whose father the place had been named. Worse yet, Muqtada al-Sadr commanded the largest and most effective insurgent militia, in this region, known as the Mahdi Army. These insurgents and others like them, with covert assistance from Iran, collected small arms for their cause. Worse yet, they regularly launched mortar rounds and rockets into the nearby Baghdad Green Zone, which originally housed Iraqi leadership, but now also served as the center for a growing international presence in the city.

Kyle and the rest of the snipers became a thirty-man special task unit charged with using tactics developed in Fallujah, Ramadi, and other battle zones to tame the insurgents of Baghdad. One conflict that had to be reconciled was differences in how East Coast and West Coast SEALs teams operated. Once that was resolved, the leadership appointed point men and other critical personnel for the missions ahead.

The army units that preceded the new crew created buffer zones with a view toward pushing the insurgents as far away from the Green Zone as possible. A tall cement fence called a "T-wall" would be constructed along a major street near the Green Zone under the protection of navy SEALs who were to exterminate as many insurgents as possible while performing guard duty. The combat engineers constructing the wall brought in concrete wall sections one at time; once each section was dropped into place, the men took turns climbing to the top and unhooking the section from the crane, often taking fire the whole time.

After an Army Special Forces Unit that had been operating in Sadr City debriefed the SEALs, Kyle and the others walked into the fire zone, thinking that this was the safest way to get started. It wasn't.

Almost immediately after they entered Sadr City, insurgents shot Kyle in the head and temporarily blinded him. Or so he thought until he realized that the shot that bloodied the top of his head knocked his helmet in front of his eyes. That wasn't the end of it because within seconds a heavy round struck Kyle in the back. Fortunately, his body armor absorbed most of the damage but left him dazed as insurgents surrounded them.

Later he remembered, "By this time, the blocks around us looked like the worst scenes in *Black Hawk Down*. It seemed that every insurgent, maybe every occupant, wanted a piece of the idiot Americans who'd foolishly blundered into Sadr City. We couldn't get into the building we retreated to. By now we'd called for a quick response force (QRF), a fancy name for the cavalry. We needed backup and extraction-'HELP' in capital letters."

Some Army Strykers, heavily armed personnel carriers, came to the rescue, firing everything they had. Potential targets, as many as a hundred insurgents, lined the roofs on the surrounding streets. Once the Strykers arrived, the insurgents changed tactics, now concentrating on army personnel carriers but were overmatched. Kyle recalled, "It started looking like video game—guys were falling off of the rooftops." Maybe half in jest Kyle said later that he heard a cavalry horn.

Two days later, Kyle's special task unit returned to Sadr City, this time in a small fleet of Strykers that dropped them at a building some five stories high filled with fruit containers and factory equipment. They quickly dubbed it the banana factory. Kyle loved the place since it provided abundant sniper hides. Kyle chose one that day on the top floor rather than the roof, which seemed too obvious and sure to draw heavy gunfire. The next morning Kyle began surveying the crowds in the streets and noticed that at about 9:00 a.m., the pedestrian and car traffic started to thin, usually a reliable sign that civilians had spotted insurgents nearby and were scattering to avoid being caught in crossfire.

All too soon, a lone Iraqi exited one of the derelict buildings, carrying an AK-47. From his vantage point, Kyle could see that this insurgent was selecting a combat engineer down the street to target and shoot. This was an easy shot, only forty yards away, so Kyle shot him dead. Another guy stuck his head out, which wasn't suspicious enough to justify shooting him under the rules of engagement (ROE) in place that day, but Kyle vowed to be on the lookout for him. Kyle called guys like this "peekers," insurgents who often knew that they could peek out of doors and windows to gather military intelligence without much risk of getting shot by the Americans.

This particular peeker decided the coast was clear, emerged with a RPG launcher in his hands, kneeled to launch it, and promptly dropped to the ground dead, thanks to Kyle. Kyle knew that eventually someone would come to retrieve the RPG. This time the RPG retriever was a small child that Kyle could have shot but chose not to, since he might have been just a curious kid.

Kyle killed another seven insurgents that day anyway and more the next day, thanks in large part to the street layout in Sadr City, his farthest shot for this series of kills was 880 yards, some were as close as 200 yards, but the average was 400, four football fields away. Kyle's kill numbers these two days were so good that he took breaks allowing other snipers opportunities to catch him. He even waived off some of the best sniper hides, thus "taking one for the team." In one abandoned house that had only a few windows, Kyle simply broke a hole in the wall, giving himself a three-hundred-yard view, a view that he didn't need that morning, since the first three insurgents walked out fifteen yards away across the street. Kyle killed them all and then offered one of the officers with him a turn.

These special task unit snipers were quick learners. Within days after beginning the Sadr City mission, they realized that the insurgents were concentrating their attacks on construction crews working near intersections. This wasn't rocket science. This insurgent tactic maximized their chances of getting away, until Kyle and the other snipers realized what was going on and took out insurgents as soon as they were spotted. There's no place to run once you're dead.

That said, Kyle and the other snipers considered Sadr City fighting more difficult than that experienced in Fallujah or Ramadi, since the insurgents brought rockets as well as AK-47s. Sniper work during the Sadr City battle mixed stress with comic relief as Kyle recalled.

"One day at the tail end of an operation, I hustled back to the Bradley with the rest of the guys. Just as I reached the vehicle, I realized that my sniper rifle had been left behind. I'd put it down in one of the rooms, then forgotten to bring it with me when I'd left. I reversed course. L.T., one of my officers was just running up. 'Hey, we gotta go back,' I said. 'My gun's in the house.' 'Let's do it,' said L.T., following me. We turned around and raced back to the house. Meanwhile, insurgents were sweeping toward it—so close we could hear them. We cleared the courtyard, sure we would run into them."

Fortunately for Kyle and the others there was nobody home, so Kyle grabbed his rifle for the race back to the Bradley and arrived just before the insurgents launched a grenade attack. Luckily, Kyle listened to the grenade explosions from inside the Bradley.

As the concrete wall project moved closer and closer to completion, the insurgent attacks began to wane, diminishing from crews of thirty to forty insurgents attacking crews at the beginning to the point where only two or three insurgents would attack the Americans when the fence was almost completed.

Coincidentally enough, by that time the insurgent leader Muqtada al-Sadr declared a cease-fire and began negotiating for peace, just as the special task unit snipers received a new assignment elsewhere. Insurgents specializing in IEDs began attacking a number of small villages outside Baghdad, coordinating their efforts with the Muqtada al-Sadr's Mahdi army even as the insurgent leader sued for peace. The

SEAL snipers began working again with snipers from the Army 4–10 Mountain Division during this new "small village" series of operations.

There were some technical differences between army and SEAL snipers to be sure. The SEALs usually spotted for themselves, while the army guys worked in pairs. Also, the army guys had fewer weapons to choose from than the SEALs. The most significant substantive differences between SEAL snipers and their army counterparts, however, were tactical. Army snipers typically conducted operations in groups of three or four, while SEAL task units often went into an area with more men and stayed longer than did their army counterparts. The SEALs thus tended to draw more attention and more attacks from the Iraqi insurgents. Kyle recalled later that the SEALs, in effect, dared the insurgents to come after them. "And they did: [in] village after village, the insurgents would come and try and kill us; we'd take them down. Typically, we'd spend at least one night and usually a few, going in and extracting after sunset."

In one particular area, Kyle and the other snipers returned to a particular village and worked out of a different house each time, killing insurgents until there wasn't anybody left.

During the three months or so that Kyle and his unit spent raiding villages, most of the houses the Americans used as sniper hides belonged to Iraqis who tried to maintain neutrality as the best means of staying alive. Curiously enough, one sure sign that a house was owned by an insurgent or an insurgent sympathizer was police uniforms that the bad guys in that region typically used to disguise themselves during attacks.

Kyle recorded some twenty confirmed kills during these missions and a routine slowly emerged. "One night we entered another village and took over a house at the edge of some large open fields, including one used for soccer. We set up [a sniper position] without a problem, surveying the village and preparing for any trouble we might face in the morning."

Kyle remembered that the conflict had slackened over the last two weeks, making him think that he might soon be heading back to his platoon running operations west of Baghdad while he set up a room up on the second floor with L.T., his spotter for the mission. "We had an Army sniper and his spotter in the room next to us and a bunch of guys on the roof. I'd taken the .338 Lapua [Magnum rifle] with me, figuring that most of my shots would be on the long side, since we were on the edge of the village. With the area around us quiet, I started scanning out farther to the next village, a little more than a mile away."

Soon enough, he spotted "a one-story house with someone moving on the roof. It was about 2,100 yards away, and even with a twenty-five power scope I couldn't make out much more than an outline. I studied the person, but at that point he didn't seem to have a weapon, or at least he wasn't showing it. His back was to me, so I could watch him, but he couldn't see me. I thought he was suspicious, but he wasn't doing anything dangerous, so I let him be." Soon he spotted a US Army convoy barreling down the road toward the American command headquarters, but now Kyle saw a problem. "As it [the convoy] got closer, the man on the roof raised a weapon to his shoulder. Now the outline was clear. He had a rocket launcher, and he was aiming at Americans."

Kyle couldn't call the convoy directly on the radio and warn them, so he did the only thing he could. "I put my scope on him and fired, hoping to at least scare him off with the shot or maybe warn the convoy. At 2,100 yards, plus a little change, it would take a lot of luck to hit him." Kyle was lucky that day. "Maybe the way I jerked the trigger to the right adjusted for the wind. Maybe gravity shifted and put that bullet right where it had to be. Maybe I was just the luckiest son of a bitch in Iraq. Whatever, I watched through my scope as the shot hit the Iraqi, who tumbled over the wall to the ground."

"Wow," I muttered.

"You dumb, lucky fucker," said L.T. Kyle killed the insurgent from 2,100 yards away, the length of twenty-one football fields end against end. "The shot amazes me even now. It was a straight-up luck shot; no way one shot should have gotten him."

"But it did. It was my longest confirmed kill in Iraq."

CHAPTER FOURTEEN

Master of the Shadows

CRAIG HARRISON AND THE MEN HE LED THAT COLD NOVEMBER DAY-break in Afghanistan drove three Jackal armored vehicles up into high ground above two miles or so south of Talajan, a village in Helmand province. They would provide observation watch and protection to a joint British and Afghanistan foot patrol clearing the village. For his part, Craig found a crumbling wall of mud and straw and positioned himself behind it with his best sniper rifle.

This seemed to be Taliban central that morning. The three-hour enemy attack just confirmed his worst fears. Wearing only a sweaty T-shirt and body armor, Craig began taking out target after Taliban target, even as he watched one of the British Jackal army vehicles hurry down into the valley to assist a foot patrol under attack from all flanks. Soon the Jackals themselves were vulnerable, trapped in a gulley, exposed to a Taliban machine gunner with an unimpaired line of sight and plenty of ammunition. Craig had seen this tactic before and knew immediately he had to take that machine gunner out. Of course, his opinion of snipers generally was hardly objective. "To my mind the sniper is the ultimate professional solder, one of the only true force multipliers in the British Army inventory. A sniper pair can wreak havoc that is completely dis-proportionate to their number. They can slow battalion advances and turn [back] attacks. They can enhance the defensive battle by making the attacker's lives living hell." Harrison added, with just a touch of pride that "we neutralize commanders and key equipment." Almost as an afterthought he added, "Snipers don't just kill though. They are trained to observe and report carry out reconnaissance and adjust mortar and artillery fire. They are the masters of the shadows."

Craig's own regiment, known as the Blues and Royals, whose proper name was the Royal Horse Guards and 1st Dragoons, originated in Oliver Cromwell's Parliamentary Army. They had no sniper tradition at all, before Harrison created one for them. Other British units, notably the Parachute Regiment, Royal Marines, and the British Special Forces carried on sniper traditions originating during World War I, reestablished during World War II, and made permanent during the 1982 Falklands War.

That cold November in Afghanistan, Craig knew that theoretically, he had no chance at all of taking out the Taliban machine gunner. His .6-ounce bullet would leave the barrel at a speed of about three thousand feet per second and take about six seconds to reach the enemy. If every variable, including wind speed, temperature, humidity, and, of all things, the rotation of the earth fell into place, he might, just might, take out the enemy he was aiming for. Never mind all that; it was time to focus.

He pushed all of the information and background noise out and focused on breathing. "As the crackle and bang of gunfire from the valley faded away, all I could hear was the thud of my heart. Through my scope I saw the gentle rise and fall of the cross hairs on the target and with each exhale I settled my aiming point on the Taliban machine gunner. Even with the magnification of the scope, the target was tiny, but I could clearly see the gunner and the weapon firing."

Later he remembered the world becoming perfectly still as he exhaled one last time before taking the shot. "I was like a statue with only the very tip of my index finger able to move. I willed my finger to start the pull and felt the briefest of resistance before the [slack] was taken up." The rifle recoiled firmly into his shoulder after he "broke" the trigger he recalled in his memoir *The Longest Kill*, the primary source for this chapter. "The scope rose off target before settling back down. Cliff, my spotter, had a telescope sight and was able to see more detail. While staring through my own scope my right ear was straining, waiting to hear what Cliff said. The seconds slowly trickled by. Count six seconds now and you will see what I mean. A lot can change in that time; most important, the target can move."

A lifetime later Cliff reported that Craig missed the target. After an expletive or two Craig started the process all over again, telling himself that he couldn't miss again.

Craig had signed up in the early nineties to take care of horses for the Blues and the Royals, known as the Queen's own "Household Calvary." That very day his older brother came home with discharge papers from the Royal Horse Artillery, which had discovered a serious hearing impairment after his enlistment. After some time on the Regimental boxing team and at a riding school in Windsor, an adventure or two with the London Police, ceremonial parades for the opening of Parliament, and routine duty guarding Buckingham Palace, Craig went absent without leave (AWOL) and tried to join the French Foreign Legion. The French promptly discovered his runaway status through an Interpol check and sent him packing back across the channel.

After serving fourteen days in military jail for going AWOL, his horse regiment transferred Craig to "P-Company" composed of men who would ultimately join the British airborne forces. Craig spared no effort getting ready for this training, spending his spare time running up thirty-two stairs in a medieval London tower and back down again, carrying a thirty-five-pound rucksack.

His first foreign assignment in the mid-nineties took him to an old abandoned building on the outskirts of Banja Luka, the second-largest city in Bosnia-Herzegovina. The British forces, working with the United Nations Stabilization Force, called the old building the Potato Factory. During this tour, Craig fired a sniper rifle for the first time. His weapon that day was a Dragunov SVD, which Craig described as an elongated AK-47. Other assignments took Craig to Macedonia and Iraq before he talked his way into becoming the first sniper in the Household Calvary.

During an earlier February 2003 tour in Iraq with a battle group that took over the football stadium at Al Amarah, Craig became acquainted with one of the snipers acting as a guard doing surveillance from the top of the structure. "He looked awesome, very, very professional, like someone that had his shit together. He was fully camouflaged. I could see that he had range cards and data sheets taped to the butt of his L96 sniper rifle. He also had a pistol in a holster and an SA80 assault rifle down by his feet."

Craig also noticed that in sharp contrast to his immaculately pristine weapons, the sniper wore clothing that hadn't been washed in weeks. "He was happy to talk, so I sat down with him and started quizzing him about being a sniper. He let me look through the scope on the rifle and I was amazed at how clear it was and how far you could see."

Craig learned that the man had been a sniper for a whole decade and asked what it takes to be a good one. The man had a faraway look in his eyes but was still willing to talk. "You make a sniper by engineering him. You go down to the essence of who he really is and then you build him back up from there, except you leave something out. You leave out the bit that says it's not okay to kill another human being. You make him into a weapon and a weapon's job is to kill people. A sniper isn't a man anymore; he is a weapon, a weapon waiting to be fired." Craig was impressed. "That's deep," Craig said. "Well, you did ask," the man said.

Over the next couple of days back at the stadium, Craig noticed that the snipers "got treated like men, not like little boys the way the rest of us were treated. They were trusted." Craig thought they were left alone to do their jobs, either as individuals or on teams. Craig thought more and more about becoming a sniper himself.

When asked what courses he would like to take once his unit returned to England, Craig got the chance he was hoping for.

He reported in mid-February 2006 for sniper training in Pirbright, Surrey, and lived the next nine weeks in a dilapidated World War II Quonset hut. Craig's first major challenge was surviving an eight-mile speed march carrying a sixty-pound pack. Twenty men dropped out that day. The instructors knew about Craig's earlier military experience taking care of horses and called him the "donkey shagger."

His first assignment after sniper school took Craig to Iraq, where he had served earlier in his first military role caring for horses. The situation now, in May 2007, was much worse. "After the initial invasion, the Iraqi Army had been disbanded, making thousands of qualified soldiers redundant and disgruntled. They soon took up arms and the insurgency—a war among the people—had continued to grow. Senior officers talked about 'reconstruction' and 'development,' but really it was survival mode now." Strangely enough, Craig embraced that which others feared. "For me it was a dream come true. Ever since my last trip to Iraq, where I'd met that sniper in the football stadium, all I had wanted to do was to deploy on operations as a sniper. Well, here I was."

Craig's first rifle while performing sniper duty was an L96, a 7.62mm weapon which had a one-thousand-yard range. The main British Army base in Iraq was in Basra. Soon however, Craig's outfit, as part of a Mobile Operation Group (MOG) attached to the King's Royal Hussars, was directed to the nearby Maysan province for a "shoot and scoot" operation in which they would engage the enemy and then pull back.

During such operations in the desert, the Royal Air Force dropped as many as ten pallets of food and water into designated zones surrounded by military vehicles with an infrared signal strobe in the center. Craig was one of two snipers assigned to this unit when a rocket attack dropped and nearly killed several men.

One type of target that Craig sought out was, in British Army lingo, a "dicker," that is to say, an informant whose job was to watch American or British military units. Dickers often operated on motorcycles and sped off with unit size and location information for the insurgents. Dickers were fair game for Craig and "Andy," the other sniper. On Wednesday morning, someone yelled the magic word.

Dicker!

Somebody pointed Craig in the right direction and he positioned himself on a sand pile. "I quickly located the dicker," Craig remembered. "It was the same guy we had been seeing for the last few days.

It was probably the same guy who called in the rocket attack." Craig chambered a bullet in his rifle and started following his new best friend. Craig had to adjust for wind and heat shimmer, not to mention that the dicker was at least five hundred yards away. Craig adjusted his scope and later talked about what happened next. "My heart was beating like mad. I could actually see my heartbeat in my cross hairs as each beat rippled through my chest. This was my first real shot as a sniper and emotions were getting the better of me. 'Slow down. Breathe,' I told myself."

He breathed deeply "and slowly exhaled, bringing myself under control. I kept taking longer breaths until my heart settled. All I was waiting for was the order to fire; I was praying that the CO [commanding officer] had some balls and would let me shoot."

He could see the glint reflecting off of the antenna on the target's radio, just as his spotter Eddy reported that the kill had been green lighted. Now Craig "settled the cross hairs onto the target—the base of his neck—and then aimed slightly lower, just so there was more target mass. The heat shimmer was really not helping, making the image swirl round my scope. I took up the slack in the trigger and held. This was it."

Bang.

Craig squinted through the heat shimmer, reloaded, and fired once more without making any target adjustments. "I could see that I had hit him with the second round as the heat shimmer died off at just the right moment."

And with that, Craig ran for his vehicle.

After a tour in Afghanistan, the British Army promoted Craig to corporal, gave him his own squad of men, and returned him to a base near Talajan, Afghanistan, in October 2009. There, he supported the Afghan National Army (ANA) and the British Yorkshire Regiment, known as the Yorks. Their living quarters were in a compound adjacent to an Afghan police station that Craig and his men fortified with sandbags and equipped with a makeshift operations room.

That November, operational orders received one morning assigned ANA troops and the Yorks to clear several Taliban compounds just south of the Talajan business district. Craig and his men were to provide overwatch, using their sniper skills to eliminate Taliban as necessary to protect the ANA and the Yorks. Craig saw this for what it was immediately: a mission to gain and maintain control of far too large an area with too few troops. Nothing as a practical matter could be done but to do the best they could.

Craig and his squad would provide overwatch from the highest terrain within the targeted area. His commanding officer gave him one solid piece of advice: think ten minutes ahead, remembering that the Taliban typically surround their adversaries in twenty minutes.

The night before the operation Craig inspected his own Jackal armored vehicle for fuel, radios, ammunition, and everything else needed for their 4:00 a.m. departure in the freezing cold. Once the three Jackals crested the high ground from which the snipers would be operating, Craig positioned them forty yards apart in an approximate circle. Now came the time to survey their situation.

After they parked, Craig climbed out of the vehicle, pulled out a map, and began absorbing the terrain as if his life depended on it. "The [targeted Taliban] compounds were the usual Afghan affair: single-story buildings, sometimes two stories, surrounded by a ten-foot wall. There was usually only one way in and out—through the single gate."

Peering through the field glasses, he could see the Yorks' patrol base as well as a triple peaked hill, almost two miles away that they would be patrolling toward. "Three Titted Hill" supported Taliban compounds and trenches. "They could sneak through this area with impunity and hit the patrol bases whenever they wanted," Craig remembered. It also allowed them to extract their wounded without being seen. The Yorks and the ANA were going to try to clear this area.

He could see a Bedouin camp about sixty yards to his right in a gully. There were the usual patches of green caused by irrigation and farming. "The whole area was crisscrossed with irrigation ditches, tree lines and low walls," Craig recalled.

Just as Craig completed his visual survey, he saw the Yorks and the ANA leaving their base to begin the operation. Within minutes, intelligence confirmed that the Taliban forces were relaying information about the Yorks/ANA operation to the very enemy units that were vulnerable. And not long after that, Craig saw a metallic glint in the distance and rugged terrain featuring high points and "dips" in the land near where Craig had halted the convoy. He ordered his driver to move their Jackal into one of the dips so that only the grenade launcher on top of the vehicle would be exposed to enemy fire. A crumbling old mud wall about twenty yards away provided a near perfect vantage point from which to watch for enemy targets.

Using his maps, a range card (chart), and makeshift wind markers consisting of light cord hanging from tent pegs, he prepared himself for those first few potential targets that might emerge from any of the thirty or so Taliban compounds he could see. The combined ANA/Yorks force now moving into the valley would surely bring some Taliban targets out into the open. Never mind that the slightest pressure on the rifle tripod perched on top of the mud wall knocked chunks of mud onto the ground and destabilized his Schmidt & Bender scope. Craig would do the best he could with what he had, leaning into the tripod and gripping it with his left hand.

Craig's primary task here was removing any dickers (observers) before they reported the combined ANA/Yorks operation to the Taliban. He had to deal with obstacles both formidable and mundane. "I was trying to get a good view through my scope but my helmet was getting in the way," Craig remembered, with some frustration. "It kept bumping in the scope and the straps were biting into my neck. I took it off and dropped it to my feet."

Finally, after a few minutes, he had a good view of all the potential targets across several compounds. "I could see Taliban stacking up behind compounds, AK47s and RPGs [grenade launchers] in their hands, clearly waiting for further directions. I was off at an angle to them and they were so focused on the patrol in the valley that they weren't paying any attention to me." Craig counted heads and estimated that he had thirty Taliban in his sights. He relayed this over to the Yorks, hoping that they wouldn't blunder into an ambush, but had his own problems.

"I needed to find the dicker," Craig told someone later. "He was the Taliban's eyes and ears and without him they were headless. It was almost 1030 hours now and the sun was shining." Once again he saw a slight glimmer off in the distance, just about where he'd seen some movement a few minutes before. "It was a long way off, almost at the base of Three Titted Hill." Something caught his eye, just left of a compound. "I focused my scope in and scanned the area. Another glint. Finally, I could see a bearded, turbaned man. The glint was coming from the antenna of the radio he was holding."

Craig tipped off Cliff, one of his fellow snipers, directing Cliff to look at the left-hand corner of Three Titted Hill, while Craig surveyed the map just beneath his seat in order to estimate the distance. Craig was sure that the dicker was at least a mile away—maybe not even within the reachable range of the rifle he would be using. Once Cliff verified the dicker location on the bottom left corner of the compound (from the sniper's elevated perspective), Craig went into the killing zone.

"I reached over and began dialing clicks into the elevation drum of my scope. When you fire a shot through a rifle, the bullet flies on a parabolic curve; it doesn't fly straight. It gains height before dropping because of gravity." Range is critical for the sniper making adjustments to compensate for the bullet's flight path.

"I dialed a massive correction into my scope. I was going to have a go. I'd never shot this far out, and from everything I'd been taught, the .338 round wouldn't go that far. You never knew though, and if I could get a round in the general area, it might keep the dicker's head down."

In extreme long-range shooting ranges, temperature, humidity, wind speed and direction, and flight time are equally critical elements. Craig explained the details better than any sniper had before. "A bullet takes around two seconds to reach 1,000 yards. That meant that, at this range, my round would be in flight for five to six seconds. During that period, the earth would have actually moved, what's known [among snipers] as the Coriolis effect. So I had to fuse all of this data together in my mind to try to make the best shot I possibly could. To start with, though, I was just going to attempt to get a shot in the right area." In Craig's preshot routine, he explained later, "I cleared my mind, regulated my breathing and concentrated on keeping the rifle as level and stable as possible. I took up the slack on the trigger and exhaled. I had the Taliban [dicker or observer]; at this range, he was a very small object in the scope, right in the center of my cross hairs." Now he got down to business. "At the peak of my exhale, I took up the 4lb of pull and the rifle barked into my shoulder. I quickly recovered from the recoil and the scope settled. I waited six seconds and didn't see anything except a very much alive Taliban. I had no idea where the shot had gone."

This time Cliff, Craig's spotter, earned his pay by estimating that the shot went in very low about 150 yards away from where it would have been effective. Craig dialed in several adjustments and sent a second bullet for the dicker's head, but the trajectory was low again. And of course they tried again. "We repeated the process eight times." The dicker had no idea that he was being targeted and probably thought what he was hearing were stray shots. "Each time Cliff spotted the impact and I made an adjustment to my scope. By the 9th shot, I had run out of clicks in the scope and was at the bottom part of the central pillar of my cross hairs. I was literally out of scope." Craig's 9th round struck the wall just below the dicker, sending the man scurrying for cover. "Finally," Craig remembered, "I was now in the field of vision for my scope so I could see where my bullets were hitting and more precisely calculate the adjustments I needed to make."

Craig fired another four rounds missing the dicker, keeping the Taliban head down without killing him, but now things became even more complicated for Craig. The good news was the British intelligence reportedly advised the sniper teams that the Taliban were chewing out the dicker Craig was firing at for not providing better intelligence on the Brits. The bad news was that two British Jackals were driving into the very center of the valley, making themselves rich targets for the Taliban. When Craig complained, he learned that this route had to be kept clear for the patrol mission that brought them here. Now Craig had three jobs, harassing or killing the Taliban dicker, providing observation overwatch for the patrol, and providing sniper cover as well.

And then the offensive kicked off. Somebody among the Yorks blew a Taliban fighter off of a roof with a grenade launcher; the valley Bedouin residents who had camels made a mad dash out of the valley, leaving their tents and everything else behind, a strong indicator that the Taliban were moving in.

All too soon, Cliff spotted two of them and adjusted his rifle scope down from a 2,000-yard range to 830 yards, stabilized the rifle on a crumbling wall, and began looking for targets. The two Taliban probably thought they were safe enough, waiting behind a wall near a compound for the British patrol to roll by. They learned that they had been flanked when Craig shot the first one in the chest, reloaded, and shot the second Taliban in the leg as he ran away. A quick head shot finished off Taliban number two, but the shadow of a 3rd Taliban on the very edge of his scope view told Craig that more actions was ahead. Taliban three crouched behind the wall of a second compound, holding an AK-47.

Craig looked at his range card and now realized that this compound was all of one thousand yards away; Craig thought that he might not have time to adjust his scope, but by the time the second Taliban arrived he was glad he made no adjustments, now realizing that the true distance was eight hundred yards away. "I kept watching and suddenly another head popped up. A second Taliban, and this one was holding an RPG. These guys definitely needed to be taken down. I settled into my rifle and controlled my breathing, exhaling and taking up the slack. I had my cross hairs on the insurgent with the RPG."

He fired but missed. "The round passing between them clearly made them jump and they started moving in different directions, the Taliban with the RPG heading into the open while the other one stayed behind the wall." Craig had plenty of time to target the Taliban in the open, so he first focused on the other one. He got off a quick shot that hit the target in the hip. "He literally spun around four times before collapsing to the ground."

Craig still had time to cross hair the guy with the RPG. "I fired. Perfect hit. His body jerked as the round slammed into him." Now Craig focused on the first target again. "There was movement back where the other guy was, his leg twitching. The hip shot had put him down but [had] not taken him out. He started trying to get to his feet, using his AK as a crutch. He was still a threat to the Yorks, so I placed my cross hairs on his chest and fired. He almost snapped in half."

Down in the valley below Craig, the patrolling Yorks were deep in the shit with small arms, machine gun fire, and RPG rounds coming in from all sides. Cliff quickly identified more turbaned targets, the best candidate being one trying to get on a motorcycle near yet another compound. Craig was quick to the scope. "I picked up a bearded Taliban with an AK-47 slung over his shoulder, settled the cross hairs on him and fired, but instantly realized that I had rushed the shot. When you shoot enough you know when a shot is good or when you have 'pulled it.'" This time Craig's round hit the bike. "The .338 bullet is big and travels with a lot of energy, so the bike slammed into the Taliban and pinned him to the floor. I cycled the bolt and fired again, hitting his left arm. He was trying to get his AK up with his right hand so I took my time, placed the cross hairs on the center of his face and fired. His head exploded, spattering the wall behind him with blood."

Craig's spotter Cliff was new to all this but didn't experience the regrets that sometimes came with first kills. This was fortunate since they were now confronted with chaos on the battlefield. The Yorks, now moving some 650 yards away from Craig and Cliff were taking fire from insurgents shooting from spaces between the buildings 100 to 650 yards in front of the approaching convoy.

And then the battle space changed. Cliff spotted an insurgent RPG team some 1,100 yards away from Craig's position getting ready to go into action against the Yorks. Craig adjusted his rifle scope by two clicks, knocked out the insurgent holding the RPG, and then knocked down a second insurgent who rushed to rescue the first. Both Taliban stayed down.

Cliff now began surveying the battle space with a high-magnification spotter scope and soon had another likely observer/informer in his sights. This time Craig dialed maximum elevation into his scope. Somehow Craig remembered the details. "Once the rifle was adjusted, I grabbed the bipod with my left hand, settled the rifle on the wall and tried to reacquire the target. 'There you are,' I muttered to myself as I spotted the same guy with walkie-talkie in the same place as before: just behind the wall. I placed the cross hairs on his chest and once I was happy that things were as stable as they could be, I fired."

Six (yes, six) seconds later, Craig watched the round strike the wall instead of the insurgent. Craig looked at the bright side, knowing that even as this particular Taliban ran away, another would soon appear. Soon Cliff reported that intelligence eavesdropping on Taliban radio transmissions discovered that a Taliban sniper was working to the left of Craig's present position. It was time to move anyway, because by this time the Taliban had either spotted Craig or knew exactly where to find him with an RPG, rifle fire, or both. Just before Craig started moving his gear, Cliff spotted an insurgent near a water pump. Craig shot that one and spotted yet another Taliban on a motorbike with an AK-47 slung over his back.

Craig gave him a "three-dot" lead, fired and missed, adjusted to a "four-dot" lead, fired a second time, and watched the targeted Taliban tumble off his motorbike. He didn't get up again, but by then the Yorks in the valley below were bogged down by intentional road flooding in the middle of Taliban central.

From their sniper overwatch perspective above the valley, they could see machine gun rounds falling all around the two Jackal vehicles from a source they couldn't identify. After a few frustrating minutes, Craig began thinking through the various enemy weapons they were facing. He remembered that the PKM, the belt-fed machine gun with the longest range, had a 1,600-yard capability. After thinking through the terrain around them, Craig concluded that the Taliban sniper must be on the Three Titted Hill. A quick scan in that direction proved that he was right. "A Taliban machine-gun team was up on the right-hand side of the compound, pouring fire down on my lads. Whereas I had been happy just to keep the dicker's head down, I knew I had to get these guys—or they were going to kill one of mine. This time the rounds had to count."

Craig started through his mental checklist, noting first that his makeshift wind markers, made up of light loose cords held in place by tent pegs, indicated that there was no wind at all. He estimated earth rotation and spin drift, checked his position to make sure he had a good "cheek weld," and got as comfortable as the conditions permitted, standing on a small incline with a rock under his right heel to keep it flat. "Finally, I was ready," Craig recalled. "I placed my aiming mark on the machine gunner, took up the trigger slack and started to exhale. I paused on the trigger's break point and a sense of calm washed over me."

He slowly squeezed and fired. "Then all I could do was watch intently through the scope for six long seconds. Miss. I cycled the bolt again. The machine-gun crew was looking around. They knew that a round had just passed very close to them. I fired again."

Six seconds later, he watched the machine gunner collapse onto his weapon. Craig didn't have time to celebrate. Telling himself to stay calm, he chambered another round, fired at the number two machine gunner, and missed, even as his target picked up the PKM and started to move out. Craig knew it was no or never for this target. He knew that everything was on the line, but that he had made all the necessary adjustments. Six seconds after firing a second time at the second Taliban gunman, he watched his target collapse on the ground.

The Yorks and their Afghanistan National Army teammates finished the patrol without further incident. It was only later that an ANA patrol confirmed that one of the machine gunners Craig killed was a local commander. An Apache helicopter hovered over Craig's firing position and used a laser range finder to confirm that the distance to the machine-gun emplacement was 2,474 meters or 2,705 yards, the length of twenty-seven American football fields end to end, the longest confirmed sniper kill in world history.

Chapter Fifteen

Six Taliban, One Bullet

You can't get much farther south in Afghanistan than Kakaran, but maybe that's what attracted Taliban insurgents to that small, remote village just north of the Pakistani border in December 2013. Or maybe it was the golden opportunity to blow up some British soldiers before they left the country that year. Whatever the reason, the Taliban insurgent might have thought that his machine gun was hidden from view that day, but as he walked along a tree line followed closely by five other suspicious men making their way toward a ditch, one of the Coldstream Guards observing him could see the machine gun partially hidden by a shawl.

The lance corporal doing sniper duty that day locked in on the Taliban wearing the shawl and shot him, hoping to see the man tumble onto the ground. Instead, the Taliban exploded with such force that the five men following him died too. And as it turned out, that Coldstream sniper probably prevented two attacks that day, since a second suicide vest was found nearby.

The contributions of the British and Canadian military to the war against terror have been significant but largely unrecognized. In fact, Canada has produced a significant number of skilled snipers disproportionate to the relatively small number of Canadians serving in Afghanistan, Iraq, and other places where good men hunt down and kill terrorists. In June 2017, the entire Canadian armed forces on active duty consisted of about seventy thousand men, as contrasted with the one million men and women on active duty in the American armed forces the previous year. And one Canadian specialty is sniping.

According to a military spokesman, on Thursday, June 22, 2017, an unidentified Canadian Special Operations sniper shot an Islamic state fighter in Iraq from 3,540 meters away, a distance that exceeded two miles, breaking the world record for distance, previously held by British sniper Craig Harrison by 1,065 meters. The fatal bullet was in the air ten seconds. Anonymous sources cited by the *Washington Post* revealed that the Canadian shot from a high-rise building was independently verified by video and was fatal.

The challenges of making such a shot seem insurmountable. Yet, *Washington Post* reporter Thomas Gibbons-Neff noted, "For the soldier to hit his target [from] 3,540 meters (3,871 yards) away, he would need to account for every atmospheric factor available. Wind speed, temperature, barometric pressure, the bullet yaw and the rotation of the earth would all have to be considered before pulling the trigger. These variables, once harnessed from devices such as a handheld weather meter and potentially range-finding equipment on the gun, would then be processed through a ballistic calculator that would let the shooter make the necessary adjustments on the rifle's scope."

A British Special Air Services (SAS) sniper made an even more difficult shot from a shorter distance in June 2018 by killing an Isis commander in Afghanistan, with an oversized 1979 vintage .50-caliber Browning machine gun from more than a mile away, using a special sight. The SAS sniper killed the standing insurgent leader as he finished a twenty-minute lecture with his men sitting around him on the ground.

Afterword

One component of future sniper operations in the war on terror may be emerging in the Helmand Province of Afghanistan, where US Marine scout snipers with Task Force Southwest began training Afghan snipers in March 2017.

Martin Pegler, the grand master of sniper literature, noted in his 2004 tome *Out of Nowhere: A History of the Military Sniper* that "the list of modern technology available to the 21st century sniper would, quite literally, fill a book of its own. Development will continue in every sphere, and training methods will constantly be improved and refined, although there seems to be little chance that for the foreseeable future sniper training will become any easier. It still remains the hardest military [specialty] in which to qualify, apart from entry into Special Forces. In a little over 100 years, the distance at which a sniper can guarantee a first round hit has risen from 300 yards to over 1,000 yards. One can speculate endlessly on what may be achieved in the next 100 years and there is no way of foretelling how an accidental discovery in one field of science may have unexpected benefits in another and where that may eventually lead. It seems unlikely, though, that the role of the combat sniper will ever be supplanted by pure technology. As one serving sniper put it, until they design a machine that works for peanuts, is totally silent, can move invisibly and get close enough to a guarantee a first round kill, my job is safe."

Chris Martin, a historian of SEAL Team Six and other works focusing on the War on Terror, has noted that American snipers are destined to remain as valuable as they've ever been. "They are tide-turning human weapons custom fit for this new age of warfare-men who can operate unseen or undercover. They are uniquely capable of operating both in preparations for larger forces or with unilateral lethality."

There will be no shortage of work for America's special operations snipers in the foreseeable future. In fact, despite making the greatest contributions of any troops throughout the Global War on Terror to date, this exceptional breed of warrior may very well prove even more critical in the next phase of that war than in the last.

Bibliography

Books

Askins, Charles. *Unrepentant Sinner.* Boulder, CO: Paladin Press, 1985.

Chandler, Norman A., and Roy F. Chandler. *Death from Afar, Vol. IV.* Jacksonville, NC: Iron Brigade, 1996.

Chandler, Roy F., and Norman A. Chandler. *White Feather: Carlos Hathcock, USMC Scout Sniper.* Jacksonville, NC: Iron Brigade Armory, 1997.

Dunkerly, Robert M. *The Battle of King's Mountain: Eyewitness Accounts.* Charleston, SC: The History Press, 2007.

Fredericksen, John. *Green Coats and Glory: The United States Regiment of Riflemen, 1808–1821.* Youngstown, NY: Old Fort Niagara Association, 2000.

Gilbert, Adrian. *Stalk and Kill: The Sniper Experience.* New York: St. Martin's Press, 1997.

Harrison, Craig. *The Longest Kill: The Story of Maverick 41: The World's Greatest Sniper.* New York: St. Martin's Press, 2016.

Henderson, Charles W. *Marine Sniper: 93 Kills.* New York: Berkley, 1986.

Ketchum, Richard M. *Saratoga: Turning Point of America's Revolutionary War.* New York: Henry Holt, 1999.

Kyle, Chris. *American Sniper.* New York: HarperCollins, 2012.

LeBleu, Joe. *Long Rifle: A Sniper's Story in Iraq and Afghanistan.* Guilford, CT: Lyons Press, 2009.

Longacre, Edward G. *The Sharpshooters: A History of the 9th New Jersey Infantry in the Civil War.* Lincoln: Potomac, 2017.

Mastriano, Douglas V. *Alvin York: A New Biography of the Hero of Argonne.* Lexington, KY: University of Kentucky Press, 2014.

McKenney, Tom C. *Jack Hinson's One-Man War.* Gretna, LA: Pelican, 2018.

Pavlichenko, Lyudmila. *Lady Death: The Memoirs of Stalin's Sniper.* Barnsley, S. Yorkshire: Greenhill, 2018.

Pegler, Martin. *Sniper: A History of the US Marksman*. Oxford: Osprey, 2007.
Saarelainen, Tapio A. M. *The White Sniper: The Deadliest Sniper in History*.
    Philadelphia and Oxford: Casemate, 2016.
Sasser, C. W., and C. Roberts. *One Shot, One Kill*. New York: Pocket, 1990.

Articles
"The 10 Deadliest Snipers of All Time," *Business Insider* (September 8, 2015).

About the Author

Laurence J. Yadon is an attorney, mediator and arbitrator, and public speaker. He has authored or coauthored thirteen books, and he has also written numerous articles and book reviews about the American West. A graduate of the University of Tulsa and University of Oklahoma College of Law, Mr. Yadon has served as a fact finder for the Department of Justice. He has been an adjunct settlement judge for the United States District Court for the Northern District of Oklahoma since 1994.